The World
At My Fingertips

Table of Contents

Table of Contents

Dedication

This book is dedicated to my loving and devoted wife, Kristi. Her unwavering support has helped give me the confidence that I can do almost anything.

To my sons, Colton and Dylan; they have given my life purpose, whether they know it or not.

To my Dad and Mom, Lamar and Janice; they have shown me unconditional love in good times and bad.

To my brother Jim and sisters Cheryl and Janice for supporting me through this difficult journey.

To my editor, Paul McNeese for helping to guide me through the publishing jungle.

Special thanks to my spiritual mentors, Dr. Travis Holcombe, and Pastors Scott Jones and Tom Schrader, for helping to light the way of my Christian walk.

And finally, to so many other wonderful family members and friends—both old and new—I would run out of room listing them here.

Foreword

Over the course of my three decades in the radio and television business I have interviewed tens of thousands of people. I feel I have learned something from each of them, but only a handful have opened the doors of my heart and stayed there. Steve and Kristi Welker not only changed me personally, but through our show, and their exceptional lives and love, they have made an indelible mark on all those who hear their story.

Before I met them, our producers had already told me about this "Ken and Barbie" couple. We were developing a show involving surrogates, and in the early 90's this was provocative stuff. I was assured that Steve and Kristi, with their good looks and fairy tale love, would win over the audience. They over-delivered! By the end of the day's taping, we were all cheering for them and their unborn twins.

Sharing time together on a TV show is an intimate thing. In many ways it is, by its very nature, a manufactured, forced event. Yet, it's a dance of trust that sometimes unfolds in an uncannily natural way. The Welkers and I seemed to know the steps the moment we said hello. Even backstage I knew that this was an important time for Kristi—to validate her journey as a beautiful young woman unable to have a biological child. Steve was less sure of this whole scene, but I could see that he would have followed Kristi to the ends of the earth. As it turned out, this stop was just shy of the Pacific, in Hollywood at my studio on the Paramount lot.

Steve was handsome beyond belief, with the kind of smile you see only in toothpaste commercials. As he told his story of using his sperm and his sister-in-law's eggs to create children who would grow in another woman's womb, the audience loved his sensitivity and openness. They were the perfect couple, pioneering a new frontier and empowering the audience along with them. Twelve years later, they are still doing that, but in a way none of us could ever have imagined.

Our staff at the Leeza Show was gathered around the production conference table when the nauseatingly horrifying news came in: our favorite guests had been in a devastating accident on the way to meet their surrogate. When Steve and Kristi's baby boys were born, Kristi was hurt so badly she couldn't hold her twins, and Steve had been blinded and couldn't see them. Cruel reality had shattered the fairy tale! Adding an unbearable twist of irony, our show featuring their happy anticipation of the birth would air just two days later.

I remember, as a pre-teen at a sleepover with my friends, that we asked each other as we gorged on junk food, "If you had to lose one of your senses what would it be?"

"Oh, I would never want to lose my sight," I said, certain that the world would be impossible without vision. When I heard about the Welker's wreck I flashed on that moment, wondering what would happen to their infant boys and what would happen to their marriage and their faith now that pain, suffering and darkness had reframed their perfect world?

On the pages of this book, my friend Steve Welker shows that real vision has nothing to do with what the physical eye can see. His story demonstrates that some questions don't have answers, and sometimes the answer is "no."

I always consider it a blessing when someone allows their story to find its way to the public through me. But, Steve and Kristi Welker did more than bless us with their story. They softened hearts and healed souls. They educated and empowered. They offered a quiet example of selflessness and hard-fought-for love that has sustained them.

There is a lot of Steve Welker that is the same as it was when I interviewed him on stage in 1994. The smile is the same. And the face, while different, is still as handsome. It is the spirit that has newly emerged. It has met up with its destiny and held hands with its purpose. This book is where he is on that path—so far.

Leeza Gibbons
Los Angeles, California
February, 2006

Introduction

It has taken me several years to get to a point in my life where I am emotionally ready to write this book. It is not that my life has been so sad that I was not able to talk about it—far from it. It was more a case of needing to be in the right state of mind to do it. I also had to be in a place where I accepted my accident and subsequent blindness, and I very much needed to be comfortable with it.

While doing the research for this book, I had to re-live, in great detail, the most difficult part of my life. Even more challenging, was asking loved ones to chronicle what was a very emotional time for them as well.

I am forever indebted to my incredible wife Kristi, my Mom Janice, and my sisters—Cheryl and Janice. They all added insight and clarity to specific situations of which I was unaware. Their perspective of the tragedy gave me a better understanding of the impact it had on others. It also allowed me to see the depth of their love and the steadfastness of their support—factors which played a critical role in my recovery.

When people hear my story, they often comment about the incredible inner strength I must have had to endure the trauma. They tell me that I surely possess a superhuman ability to overcome incredible odds and persevere. The truth is, I am an average guy that has been through a horrific event and I just took the path that seemed the most logical.

After living through the tragedy and feeling all the emotions of dismay, disillusionment and discouragement, I came to the realization that I had but two choices: I could either crawl into my bedroom and never leave (and believe me, there were days when that was exactly what I wanted to do), or I could pick up the pieces of my life and move on.

What I am trying to convey is this: I believe most people, when they truly accept their limitations, can develop or uncover from within themselves an ability to overcome great odds. Superhero status is not a prerequisite. One does not have to possess indefatigable willpower or unshakeable motivation to succeed after a tragedy. With the proper tools and faith in God, most people can do it.

Several years ago, I listened to a book written by W. Mitchell entitled *It's Not What Happens to You . . . It's What You Do about It.* The author says, before his accident there were 10,000 things he *could* do. Afterwards, there were only 9,000. He realized that he could either focus on the 9,000 things he *could* still do or the 1,000 that he couldn't. Like W. Mitchell, I choose to focus on the things I *can still do.*

As time has passed, I have realized that the vast majority of us have one sort of disability or another. While many of these afflictions are not readily visible—conditions like personality disorders, addictions or various health problems—they are no less debilitating than my blindness. I hope my story can help these people see that there is a light at the end of the tunnel. I have *chosen* to recognize my limitations and accept them. I've had to find new ways of doing almost every task in my life, and there are many things I would love to do but simply *can't.* My motto has become "It is what it is."

On the flip side of the coin, my blindness and subsequent rehabilitation have put me in a position to experience many things I never could have experienced before my accident. I frequently do motivational speaking about my life. I've served for several years on Boards of Directors for various social service agencies. I have had an opportunity to meet prominent businesspeople, professional athletes, celebrities and, most importantly, many wonderful individuals who have dedicated their lives to improving the human condition.

Public speaking has given me the opportunity to meet others who struggle with grief and trauma and want answers to their problems. They question why things happen and what they can do about it. My hope, as you read my life story, is that you will perceive it as a triumph of the human spirit and realize that with God's help, you too can overcome. With that knowledge, anything is possible.

Steve Welker
Phoenix, Arizona
May 2006

Part One:

"The Lord is my shepherd . . ."

Chapter 1

Life Before the Storm

April 30, 1994 dawned bright and clear. It was one of those beautiful spring days in Phoenix. The sky was a perfect powder blue and there wasn't a cloud in it. My wife, Kristi, and I were very excited, but nervous, as we headed to the airport. How we had gotten to this heady place in our lives seemed more like a dream than a reality.

We had married almost two years earlier. During our courtship Kristi informed me she'd had a hysterectomy many years before and would never be able to carry a child. I felt so fortunate to find this amazing woman that this news really didn't bother me. I figured we would adopt a baby at some point and that would be that.

Then, one day in early 1993, Kristi came home from work—at the time, she was working as a pharmaceutical sales representative for Bristol-Myers Squibb—with a rather intriguing offer.

"Honey," she asked excitedly, "do you remember that medical assistant, Terri Jenkins, who works for one of the physicians that I call on?"

I replied that I didn't, but the name sounded familiar. You see, Kristi has one of those 'Midwestern' personalities. She meets no strangers and gets to know them in about five seconds. The significant amount of personal information they share with her never ceases to amaze me.

"Well," she continued, "Terri has offered to be our surrogate. Can you believe it?"

"Really? That's great," I responded, having no idea what a surrogate was. Remember, this was 1993 and the concept was rather new. I figured it was someone that was going to help us around the house with the laundry and dishes and other household duties. Sounded great to me.

After moving to a spot right in front of me so she was sure she had my full attention, she tried again. "I don't think you understand. Terri has offered to carry a baby for us."

I was perplexed. We didn't have a baby. After several minutes, Kristi finally managed to get through to me what Terri had offered.

"Does her husband know about this proposition?" I asked.

As it turned out, he was well aware and fully supported the idea. Terri and J.J. already had four children of their own and they thought Kristi and I deserved to be as blessed as they were.

It took several more minutes for Kristi to explain to me, slowly and simply, a procedure called in-vitro fertilization (IVF).

The process entails the eggs being removed from a donor, injected with sperm, and placed in a Petri dish in an incubator (an "Easy Bake Oven," as it was explained to me). If the procedure is successful, the sperm fertilizes some of the eggs and forms embryos, which are then implanted into the surrogate's womb. From that point on, it is usually a normal pregnancy.

Now remember, this is a non-medical guy's simplified version of a complex procedure. Left out of it are details like the hundreds of injections and various medications the donor and the surrogate have to endure. And, the actual egg retrieval and the implantation is no piece of cake, either.

Included in this progression, it turned out, was an incredible amount of psychological testing. The surrogate, egg donor and mother to be were all given extensive written tests and one-on-one interviews. Oddly, I was not pre-qualified. I guess they figured anyone could be a father; for that job the bar seemed to be set fairly low.

Being the left-brained, logical-thinking person that I am, I couldn't really imagine this venture succeeding with a baby—our baby. There were entirely too many emotional, physical, legal and financial barriers to overcome. But I figured, "What the heck, we'll run down this road until we hit the first insurmountable wall, then we go back to plan A." Over the course of our still-short relationship, I had already discovered that Kristi was a bit of a dreamer. I assumed this adventure fell into that category and would soon run its course.

The next improbable ingredient we needed for this unlikely scenario was an egg donor, so Kristi called her sister Karla in Joplin, Missouri. Karla was married and already had two children of her own. She, too, thought it would be wonderful if Kristi and I could be parents. After discussing this with her husband, Mark Tyrrell, they agreed to help us out. No minor decision!

Our next major hurdle was the financial one. Being a conservative businessman, I thought this one would kill the deal for sure. This process was not cheap, and we would need to borrow some of the money from somewhere—but where?

After exhausting all of the usual sources with little success, I resigned myself to the notion that our dream was gone. Then Kristi came up with a completely ridiculous idea: her grandfather could loan us the money. Her stingy, penny pinching, stubborn and slightly ornery grandfather, who was a very successful rancher in Missouri and who, in a hundred years, would never understand this complex, modern medical procedure. Loan us money? No way! Against my better judgment, we flew to his ranch house to pay him a visit. On the following afternoon, after about 15 minutes of discussing the idea in his living room, he agreed to lend us the money!

Apparently, ranchers had been artificially impregnating cattle for years, and he didn't think our plan seemed all that strange. Go figure.

In my practical mind, the funding was only the second-biggest hurdle we had to overcome. The first, of course, was the process itself, which seemed absolutely impossible to me. It struck me more as magic than as medicine.

In October of 1993, the four of us—Terri, Karla, Kristi and I—headed off for San Francisco, California, to the Pacific Fertility Clinic of Dr. Geoffrey Sher. Karla brought along her 17-month-old daughter, Taylor, and the party was on.

As a cost saving measure, I put us in a single hotel suite. Now, I know what you may be thinking: given the extremely high levels of hormones and progesterone in that room, there must have been a lot of whining and complaining going on. To be completely honest, I think most of that was coming from me!

Our initial visit to the clinic was, well, odd. We all sat in a conference room with our doctor while he explained the IVF procedure. He calmly went on about it, making it sound much like we were going to bake a cake or a tin of muffins. He actually made the whole thing intelligible to me, and I began to think that it might be possible to do it successfully . . . maybe.

From that point on, we waited for the best possible time in the cycles for egg retrieval and embryo implantation. When that time came, my sperm was injected into the eggs that had been retrieved from Karla, placed in a Petri dish, and put in an incubator. After a day or so, the viable embryos were injected into Terri's uterus. All told, we spent ten days in California.

We then returned to Phoenix and waited. It took about two weeks to determine whether or not we had a viable pregnancy. It was a very anxious time for Terri, Kristi and me. We all tried, with great difficulty, to act like everything was normal. But it wasn't. It was a bit like waiting to see if we'd won the lottery.

One thing I knew for certain during those suspenseful hours . . . I had, in a sense, already won *my* lottery—I had Kristi, and she loved me.

Miracle of Miracles—Kristi!

How Kristi and I met is a bit of a miracle in and of itself. I'd reached a point in my life where I had begun to think I would never find the right woman. It wasn't that I was trying to find a perfect woman: just one I could connect with on a deep emotional level.

I was 34 years old, had never been married, and had nearly convinced myself that marriage might not be in the cards for me. I believed I would make a good husband, but it just hadn't happened. Then, just as I was resigning myself to the sad fate of eternal bachelorhood, Kristi Kelley exploded into my life.

I saw the truth to the old adage that says, "When you quit looking for something, that's when you'll find it."

Kristi and I were introduced by a mutual friend, Angie Milliken, but it wasn't a typical match making set-up at all. In fact, Angie had two of my friends in mind and was trying to fix Kristi up with one of them. Seems she had never thought of me. Coincidently, though, as Angie's plot was unfolding, I just happened to be around.

It was another one of my usual Friday nights, in late June of 1991, at Houston's, an upscale restaurant in the Phoenix area. I had been meeting my buddies there every Friday night for longer than I care to admit. I was anticipating just another uneventful night in a long chain of uneventful nights. As it turned out, I was about to find what I had been looking for.

When I was introduced to Kristi, I felt an immediate, strong attraction. Kristi is a beautiful lady, which intimidated me a bit at first. But after a few minutes of conversation I began to feel at ease and see she was really down to earth. I remember thinking, "She has every right to be one of those stuck-up model types you run into, but she isn't." As this thought ran through my mind, Kristi told me that she had recently moved to Phoenix from the Midwest and was just getting settled in the big city. These two facts were enough for me—they explained her honest, friendly attitude.

As we spoke, I nervously tried to come off as witty and as charming as I could. I thought that I failed miserably, but it was no great loss because I really didn't think I had a chance with her, anyway. Besides, Kristi was there to be introduced to a couple of other guys, not me—and she knew that. As far as I knew, I wasn't even on her radar screen. To top it off, Kristi was gorgeous—way out of my league.

Our group decided to have dinner at Hops, a trendy new restaurant in Scottsdale. As is so often the case with bellwether restaurants, there was a long line to get in. My friends and I arrived a few minutes before Kristi and Angie. As I tried to engage in small talk with my buddies, I kept glancing toward the parking lot to see if Kristi was going to show up.

I still don't know where they parked, but all of a sudden, there was Angie beside me, whispering into my ear that Kristi was interested in me. "What makes you say that?" I asked, as casually as possible even though my heart seemed to accelerate to a thousand beats a minute as I was trying not to break into a huge grin.

"Well," she said, "on the way over here, I asked her who she liked, Stan or Rich—and she said, 'Steve'."

As you can tell, I am not usually an overly confident man when it comes to the ladies. But once I wrapped my mind around Angie's inside information, I found myself much more confident and I vowed to get to know Kristi better—right away!

As our large party was finally seated for dinner, I maneuvered myself to sit next to Kristi. I could see that the other two guys had the same idea, but somehow or another, there I was, sitting directly to her right at the table. Later, of course, I found out that Kristi was trying to sit next to me, too, which, unbeknownst to me, had made it a 'slam-dunk'.

Throughout the dinner, Kristi and I pretty much ignored the rest of the table and talked only to each other. Every once in a while, one of the guys would try to get her attention with a witty line, but they were unsuccessful. There was definitely electricity—or at least fantastic 'chemistry'—passing between us.

In the first few minutes of our conversation, we discovered that we shared the same birthday, July 9th. At first, Kristi thought I was making this up to impress her. I had a feeling I was starting to lose her already, so I awkwardly produced my driver's license as proof, and in that moment we both started to feel like our meeting was more than just a coincidence. Fate was stepping in, and we both knew it.

As the evening wound down, I knew I just had to see Kristi again as soon as possible. I had previously planned to fly to Las Vegas the next morning with my friend Dino Paul. In as nonchalant a manner as I could muster, trying to make it look as though I did this all the time, I asked Kristi if she wanted to go with us.

Unfortunately, she said, she couldn't make it because she already had a date with another guy. Needless to say, I figured she must be so popular that she had a date every day of the week and I really didn't stand a chance with this gorgeous girl. My head was telling me, "Oh, well, it was fun while it lasted."

Dino and I met at the airport the next morning, but fate stepped in again and we two 'stand-by flyers' were unable to catch a flight. Not wanting to sound too desperate, I waited until that afternoon to call and ask her out for the next night. I was really eager to see her again and absolutely ecstatic when she said, "Yes."

Our first date was a basic 'dinner and a movie gig', but it was the best date of my life. When I picked her up, she was unusually eager to introduce me to her dog, a toy Pomeranian named Panda. Actually, that worried me a little, but at least I had enough self-confidence to assume that the dog didn't represent any romantic competition. What I soon learned was that Kristi used Panda as a 'boy barometer'. Panda, was very special to Kristi. I had a feeling that Panda's response to meeting a new man would dictate Kristi's level of involvement. Fortunately, Panda and I got along great. Kristi later told me that if Panda hadn't liked me, it would have been our last date.

On our second date, the Fourth of July, I got a little more creative. I took her to a Garth Brooks concert on the Fourth of July. I'm not a huge country/western fan, but I was already a Kristi Kelley fan. At the end of the concert, as fireworks were bursting overhead, we shared our first kiss. I know it sounds corny, but it was very intense, a moment I will never forget. It was one of those flash points when you *know* that something life-changing has just taken place. After that special evening, our future together looked bright, indeed, and we never looked back.

A few days later, Kristi left for Princeton, New Jersey to attend a month-long training session for a medical supply company in which she'd just been hired. This separation, occurring so soon after we met, really helped us to get to know each other better; we would talk on the phone for hours every evening about anything and everything. My long-distance bill that month rivaled the national debt.

One night, I made the mistake of calling her for one of our extended telephone sessions when my friends Bob Schaefer and Dino Paul were over. I should have known better than to leave those two alone without adult supervision, but I was smitten and I wasn't thinking too clearly.

As I sat in another room talking to Kristi on the phone, I suddenly heard them screaming, and my nostrils detected the unmistakable smell of smoke.

When I'd left to make my call, they were playing with my new electric race-car set. Fueled by too many beers, they decided it would be cool to see if they could build a ring of fire for the cars to jump through. Tightly twisted paper towels doused with charcoal lighter fluid would do the trick, they agreed. As I entered the room, they were dumping their beers on the fire, which had gotten a little out of control. Right then and there I decided that I was growing tired of my bachelor life.

A year later, I did the smartest thing I have ever done in my life, I married Kristi. On July 11, 1992 we exchanged our wedding vows at the Tropicana Island Wedding Chapel in Las Vegas, Nevada. It was the only time I have ever left that town a winner. I had Dino run the video camera at the wedding and reception. I figured it was the least he could do for me, considering that he nearly burned down my house.

Chapter 3

The Pregnancy

In November of 1993, Terri, Kristi and I went to our obstetrician for the first ultrasound. After what seemed like an hour of searching, the nurse gave us the blessed news: we had a viable pregnancy. Although we were still in the very early stages and fully aware that there were many possible hazards ahead of us, we were on cloud nine. My feet didn't touch the ground as I walked out of the office. On the drive home with Kristi, I finally admitted to myself that the whole incredible plan might work.

I am normally the sort of person who does not accept success until it is literally in the bank. So it was most unusual that even at this early, precarious time, I firmly believed that the odds of us getting a baby were good. "You see?" I joked with Kristi. "I told you this would work. Nothing to it."

Terri's pregnancy was classified high-risk because of the IVF. She needed to have an ultrasound every two weeks. While we were not as nervous at our second visit, the tension remained high; there were still so many things that could go wrong. During that session, when the nurse told us that she was hearing a second heartbeat, my mind raced. "What does this mean? Does our baby have two hearts?" My confusion was soon cleared up when the nurse excitedly announced, "It looks like twins!"

How fortunate could we be? Kristi and I had already agreed that this was going to be our only attempt at this. We had decided that the emotional roller coaster we had been on—not to mention the financial cost—was something we couldn't go through again, nor could we ask Terri or Karla to endure the painful procedure a second time.

We had heard stories of couples who were absolutely obsessed with having their own babies and we agreed we were not in that state of mind. If this didn't work the first time, we would adopt.

So here we were with twins on the way. God had blessed us with a chance at a family in one fell swoop. We were, quite obviously, on top of the world.

On a regular basis, we continued to go for ultrasounds. By now, we were having them performed at a hospital close to Terri and J.J.'s home.

Our first hospital visit was rather interesting. Because this was a "normal" maternity ward, the staff was not accustomed to our unique situation. Four people having two babies? The staff tried to prevent Kristi and me from entering the room, declaring it was reserved for parents only. They were rather dumbfounded when Terri told them Kristi and I *were* the parents. After several minutes of explaining our exceptional situation and how we all fit into it, they reluctantly agreed to allow all of us to be in the room while the ultrasound was done. The room was exceptionally small, but we all fit in there—Terri, J.J., Kristi, the nurse, and me.

Eventually, we settled down to our every-other-week routine and quickly became mini celebrities at the hospital. As the staff became familiar with our story, they really got on board.

Watching those fuzzy black and white ultrasound videos of our babies is forever imprinted in my mind. The way we could watch them moving and stretching, making fists with their little hands and even kicking each other, was truly amazing. I'm sure the fact that these are the only times I ever saw my sons helps to intensify the images in my mind.

Fathers-to-be are often asked what they want to have, a boy or a girl. In my case, I can honestly say I truly didn't care. I felt that being blessed with not one but two babies was more than I could have possibly asked for or even dreamed of.

I seem to remember, in the back of my mind, I thought a boy and a girl would be the best arrangement. You know, one of each.

After only a few months, it quickly became apparent that baby A was most definitely a boy. I boasted to everyone, "The apple doesn't fall far from the tree!" Kristi's giggling in the background didn't help, I can assure you.

As we went in for subsequent visits, I was secretly hoping to discover a girl in the baby B slot. Kristi is such a beautifully feminine woman; I knew she would make a great mom to a daughter. She was a natural for the emotional attachment that often exists between a mother and daughter. She also would have been great at all of that girly stuff, like getting dressed-up, putting on make-up, cooking and shopping.

Now, don't get me wrong. I am not a male chauvinist. I believe in equality in the work place and all that, but I also believe that there is a difference between the sexes and that God intended it to be that way. Not that a man can't cry, or a woman can't change a tire, but let's not go overboard, OK?

In about the sixth month, our ultrasound technician gave us the news we had all been anticipating. Baby B was also a boy. My disappointment that Kristi was not going to get her little girl was quickly replaced with the elation that we were going to have two boys! How cool was that?

I tried to hide my excitement. Two boys to play ball with, two boys to collect baseball cards with, two boys to take fishing and skiing, and two boys to take to the ball games. This being a dad thing was going to be great!

Kristi was far from disappointed with this news. She, like me, would have felt blessed with two boys, two girls, or one of each.

In retrospect, God knew just what he was doing when he gave us boys. (Doesn't He always?) Kristi has turned out to be the best boy mom in the world. They have toughened her up a bit, and she has given them the polish and manners that are all too rare among boys today.

ß

As you might expect, our unusual situation brought us quite a bit of attention. Our pre-natal Lamaze classes proved to be quite entertaining. Terri, Kristi and I would come in, grab our pillow, and have a seat on the floor. The other moms and dads didn't quite know what to make of us. No matter how crowded the class was, they all steered clear of the area where we were sitting. It seemed as though they didn't want to get too close to us. They probably thought we were some new-age family—or perhaps 'hangover hippies'. Nothing could have been further from the truth. During this stage, we were often asked if we intended to explain to our boys the nature of their unique birth. Kristi and I were in total agreement. I would sit them down for a little father-to-sons talk, look them right in the eyes and say, "Boys, your mother has something very important she wants to tell you."

We also attracted the attention of the Leeza Gibbons show. Leeza wanted to do a unique human-interest story on this controversial procedure called surrogacy. Her producers contacted the Pacific Fertility Clinic, and the staff told her about us. Leeza loved the story idea of a woman donating her eggs so her sister could have a baby.

Within a couple of weeks, a producer contacted us with an invitation to appear on the talk show. We were going to be on national TV, all because of Kristi's improbable dream. So, it was off to Hollywood. The taping of the show proved to be a lot of fun. We were featured for the entire hour and the staff made us feel like real celebrities.

Leeza was not at all what I expected. I anticipated that she would be a phony, Hollywood type. I guess, in general, I really don't have much respect for that entire industry, so naturally I assumed she wouldn't even meet my low expectations. The only reason we agreed to do it, I rationalized, was to help educate infertile couples about the exciting options of IVF and surrogacy. At the beginning of the show, Leeza had Kristi and me tell our amazing story. Then she introduced Terri and Karla, who talked about their generous contributions for these miracles in the making. Ultrasounds of the babies were then shown.

As I sat there on stage, I couldn't believe all of this was really happening. Mere words cannot begin to describe the depth of gratitude and appreciation I felt for these incredible women whom God was using to create our little miracles. The fact that Karla and Terri had gone through so much—both emotionally and physically—just so Kristi and I could have children of our own was beyond what my mortal mind could comprehend. I realized at that point that I would never be able to adequately thank them for these gifts of love.

Later in the show, Leeza even went into the audience to interview the husbands, J.J. and Mark. Then, Dr. Geoffrey Sher from the Pacific Fertility Clinic appeared and discussed the medical aspects of IVF. As a special surprise, they presented a woman named Linda Mack. Linda had been through a situation similar to ours and had acted as a mentor to

Kristi through our pregnancy. Her advice and support was incredibly helpful to us. (Unfortunately, several years later, Linda lost her life in a boating accident).

After the taping, we all relaxed in the green room (Yes, there really *is* a green room, but at Leeza's show it wasn't green). It was all rather surreal—not only the successful IVF, but also that we had just taped a national TV program. Best of all, I judged that I hadn't said anything too stupid or embarrassing. I joked that I was pretty sure Leeza had a crush on me. I couldn't wipe the silly smile off my face for the rest of the day.

From the moment we arrived on the set I was as high as a kite. I remember Kristi teasing me for making goofy faces and watching the taping through the video monitors while I was on stage. (Little did we know that this would be the only time I would see the show). Leeza was very warm and friendly to us. She knew our entire story. She spent quite a bit of time with us before the show and chatted casually between takes. No question about it, she took a personal interest in who we were. As time and events unfolded, she turned out to be a true friend and supporter. Once again, my pre-conceived notions were significantly off the mark.

After we returned to Phoenix, the final, nervous segment of the pregnancy got into full swing.

ß

Naming our boys turned out to be a process of elimination. I established quite a few 'rules'. For instance, I didn't want any names that started with the same letter—like Kyle and Kenny. I thought this would be too corny. I didn't want our sons to have names that sounded like they belonged in a Kodak commercial. Also, no names that could be easily modified on the playground into an embarrassing nickname, like Earl (Hurl), Zeke (Geek), or Nick (well, you get the point).

Frustrated at my inflexibility, Kristi eventually got her hands on a book filled with boys' names. I think there were at least a thousand names in it. After a long, arduous process, I finally agreed on three potential names, Colton, Connor or Dylan. Frankly, I was surprised I found so many acceptable. Dylan was in, due to the previously mentioned rule regarding names beginning with the same letter. We eventually settled on Colton. I thought it sounded very western, very modern. That makes sense, doesn't it?

Baby A was now officially Dylan and baby B was Colton. It was a good thing we assigned the boys their names in advance, because our plans to be there for their birth didn't come to fruition.

The Lord blessed us with lots of friends, and as a result, we had four baby showers. The dozens and dozens of items we received to clothe, feed, entertain and take care of these tiny babies filled every available space in our home. I don't think General Patton required as much equipment to invade Europe!

The nursery was quite an ordeal. First, we had to find wallpaper and a border that met my strict requirements. You see, much like the naming issue, there were many items on my "unacceptable list." For instance, no corporate logos (Disney, Warner Bros., etc.), no smiley faces, no kids with balloons, no loud colors. Kristi once again tolerated my rigid demands. We finally decided on bunny rabbits playing on a teeter-totter. For the record, they were very macho bunny rabbits wearing cowboy hats—and the colors were muted tans, beige and peach.

The project of hanging wallpaper was, well, worthy of note. As a result of this exercise, I have a recommendation for marriage counselors: a session on installing wallpaper together should be included in all courses offered to couples contemplating marriage. If the couple can successfully do this, then they can get through anything! Luckily, Kristi and I successfully completed the project. She let me oversee the job, said nothing when I put the border upside down, and never commented on my glaring mistakes. What a woman!

During this time, we became very close to Terri's family. They had four children: two boys and twin girls. We got together with them almost every weekend. It was more like being with friends than being with the woman who was carrying our twins. Most of the time, we didn't talk about—or even think about—the situation that had brought us together. The few occasions when it did come up were usually times when Kristi and I were worried about Terri's health. We tried to keep her on the couch at all times, and we constantly asked her how she felt.

Terri, bless her heart, humored us and tried to keep us calm. After all, she had been pregnant before. We had not.

One day, we went to a place called Castles & Coasters, an amusement park, with the entire Jenkins family. At the time, Terri was almost seven months pregnant and as big as a house. The park offered a variety of roller coasters, bumper cars and other rides that Kristi and I tried our best to steer Terri away from. Every time she even looked in the general direction of those dangerous machines, we found a reason to herd her the opposite way. Basically, our plan was to do our very best to keep her in the air-conditioned snack bar eating only healthy food. (We were sure that hot dogs would cause some permanent birth defect.)

To her credit, Terri had no intention of riding any of the rides, and her choice of foods that day was above reproach. Kristi and I were nervous parents-to-be, while Terri was as cool as a cucumber. As I said, it was our first pregnancy; it was Terri's fourth.

Happily, Kristi and I managed to survive the pregnancy just fine. I didn't sleep well for several weeks and my stomach was twisted in knots for days at a time, but I managed to get through it.

℞

On the afternoon of April 29, 1994, we had the biggest scare of the pregnancy. Terri had been complaining of cramping for several weeks, and for the most part she had been restricted to bed rest. We were only seven months into the pregnancy, and it was looking as though it would be a real battle to keep the babies from coming early.

On this otherwise mild and mostly sunny afternoon, J.J. called to advise us that Terri was severely cramping and that he thought she might be going into pre-term labor. We agreed to meet them at St. Joseph's maternity ward, where Terri was admitted for observation.

The stress of that afternoon and evening was unbelievable. J.J. and I waited for hours in the waiting room while the hospital staff monitored Terri. Kristi stayed with her, returning to the waiting room periodically to give us updates. The doctors administered a drug to delay labor, and Terri was kept as still as possible.

After seven hours, the staff determined that Terri was out of danger, at least for the moment. Later that night, we decided to move to the next phase of our plan.

In the early stages of our surrogacy discussions, we discovered that we had somewhat of a legal obstacle to overcome. At that time (1994), the state of Arizona had not yet recognized all of the possible biological implications of IVF.

The state viewed the woman giving birth as the mother, regardless of the origin of the eggs. There were no exceptions to the law. Furthermore, the letter of the law considered the husband of the woman giving birth to be the father, regardless of the origin of the sperm.

While this entire process would not have been possible without both Terri and J.J., neither of them was in any way biologically related to our sons. Yet, on the birth certificates of our babies, according to Arizona law, Terri would be shown as the mother and J.J. as the father. Since none of us were comfortable with that, we started looking for options.

Fortunately, the State of California was ahead of the curve on this issue, which seemed to offer us a solution. There, a procedure was in place that specifically addressed IVF births. We petitioned the California court in advance of the births, advising them of the egg and sperm donors. Furthermore, we had Karla legally donate the eggs to us. As a result, Kristi's name would show on the birth certificate as the mother and mine as the father. In order for that to be the case, though, the babies would have to be born in California.

Once again, a certain power was looking out for us. As it happened, Terri's Aunt lived in California, within blocks of a very highly respected hospital with a maternity ward and full facilities to handle high-risk pregnancies. After our scare with the possible premature delivery, we re-set our timeline and decided to send Kristi and Terri to California the next morning. Then, as soon as Terri went into labor, I would hop on the next flight and join them.

Things were still moving in the right direction. We were actually feeling fairly confident. We had planned for every likely obstacle, and even for every un-likely one—or so we thought.

Part Two:

"Yea, though I walk through the valley of the shadow of death . . ."

Chapter 4

The Accident and Its Aftermath

So there we were, heading out the door of our Tempe home on that beautiful April day to meet Terri at the Phoenix airport. We loaded Kristi's bags in the back of my Jeep Cherokee. I threw in my basketball gear, as I had planned to play hoops for a while after I dropped her off.

We headed first for a nearby Wal-Mart store to pick up some new contact lenses for Kristi. On the way, we got into a silly little argument over the need to endorse some checks that I was to deposit into our account. I asked Kristi to endorse them, but she worried that it wasn't safe to sign checks before I got to the bank, since someone could cash them if they were lost or stolen.

"What could possibly happen?" I protested. What, indeed!

By the time we got to Wal-Mart, I had used my sense of humor to defuse the situation. We were soon laughing about the whole thing, and before we went into the store she endorsed the checks.

I remember being in a great mood, holding her around the waist as we walked through the parking lot to the entrance of the store. It was one of those times of feeling vibrant and alive. That was to be my last conscious memory for the next two weeks. .

After we left Wal-Mart, we planned to make one more stop before the airport. Kristi had ordered a mother's ring for Terri. We wanted to pick it up from the jewelry store and give it to her before she and Kristi boarded the California-bound jet. But we never made it.

We were northbound on 68th Street in Scottsdale, both nervous and excited about the world around us. And then, in an instant, our lives were forever changed.

The following description of events has been conveyed to me. I have no memory of them.

Shortly after we had turned onto 68th Street from Curry Road, we saw a southbound vehicle coming toward us, slowly pursued by a police car. As soon as I noticed the flashing lights of the police car, I pulled my Jeep Cherokee all the way over to the right and even up onto the sidewalk. We then waited for the pursuit to pass us and continue south. Unfortunately, the vehicle suddenly accelerated, veered to its left, jumped the center median, careened across the northbound lane of 68th Street, and hit us head-on at nearly 60 miles an hour. We later found out that the vehicle had already sideswiped another car, which was the event that precipitated the police chase.

The preliminary conclusion was that the driver had begun to slip into a diabetic coma but apparently thought he was still able to operate the vehicle. Further investigation revealed that this was his third auto accident under such circumstances in less than two years.

The weight and momentum of the other vehicle, a large sedan, was too much for our Jeep to withstand. The collision nearly demolished our car, throwing it into the air and flipping us over several times. We finally landed, upside-down, in the middle of 68th Street, with the A-frame of the passenger compartment collapsed around us.

Kristi was trapped inside our vehicle, lying on the crushed, twisted metal ceiling. Unfortunately, she does have some recollection of the horrific moments after the collision, but she was fading in and out of consciousness. As she lay there, trapped upside down, she recalls some helpful passerby trying to comfort her. He was also advising her to tell me to lie down.

In shock, I had somehow gotten out of the Jeep and was attempting to direct traffic, even though my head was bleeding from the severe impact I had absorbed from the steering column, the splintering dashboard and the collapsing roof of the Jeep.

Ironically, a couple of weeks prior to our accident, Kristi and I had been among the first to come upon another auto accident. At that time, I had ended up directing traffic at a busy intersection for nearly a half-hour because the police were busy tending to the injured drivers and passengers. I think that sub-consciously I went back to that day and tried to pick up where I left off.

When the paramedics arrived at the scene of our accident, they were able to cut Kristi from the wreckage. She was taken by ambulance to Scottsdale Memorial Hospital, less than five miles from the scene. Upon initial examination, the doctors determined that she had suffered a crushed left foot, closed head injuries, and breaks in both of her collarbones.

Kristi tells me that she continued to fade in and out of consciousness during her trip to the hospital and in the emergency room. She says, all she could really think about was my condition. After she asked time and again if I was okay, without getting any answers, she assumed that I had not survived.

I was flown by medical helicopter from the accident scene to Maricopa County Hospital. We later learned that in situations with multiple 'trauma level 1' patients it was normal procedure to take them to separate hospitals so that the emergency staffs would not be over-taxed.

Within minutes of my arrival the medical staff recorded that I had broken virtually every bone in my face, was bleeding from multiple lacerations, and my right eye had been badly damaged. I was conscious and talking, but it has never been determined if I still had vision in my left eye. In those critical first hours, the primary medical concern was to save my life.

ᛩ

My sister Cheryl was the first family member to arrive at the hospital, approximately three hours after the accident. By this time I was unconscious, anaesthetized and lying battered and beaten in my bed in the Surgical Intensive Care Unit (SICU). The portion of my face not covered by bandages was badly swollen and discolored. Oxygen tubes trailed from my nostrils. Intravenous lines and an assortment of electrical monitoring devices punctured or surrounded me from head to waist. The only way Cheryl could identify me was by inspecting my familiar hands, which she set down and held tightly.

The nurse read from my file and began cataloging my injuries to Cheryl, who didn't really understand most of the medical terminology. But it was transparently clear that I was in bad shape. More importantly, she knew the nurse was preparing her to understand that I might not make it.

After that, as the nurse went about her duties, Cheryl continued to hold my hands and talk to me. She told me everything was going to be all right, that we would get through this, and that Kristi was OK. The nurse told Cheryl it was important to keep talking to me, because often times the unconscious patient will hear these words of encouragement. I don't know whether I did or not, but Cheryl remembers that I grew a bit calmer as she talked to me. After a while, a nurse told Cheryl they had to take me for more tests.

During the entire process, Cheryl had noticed a young police officer sitting behind the nurse. She thought it curious that he just sat, listened, and watched what was happening. After I had been wheeled off, the officer stood, took Cheryl by the arm and escorted her down the hall to a small desk. Along the way, he explained he was the lead investigator for the accident and it was standard operating procedure for him to personally notify a family member. Obviously, this was no ordinary traffic accident.

After he finished telling her the details of the accident, he took her to a social worker. As they walked, he asked, "Are you a nurse?"

"No", she answered, "I'm a banker. Why do you ask?"

"You seem so calm" he responded, "I thought you saw this kind of thing all of the time."

"No" Cheryl said, "I'm just in shock and don't know how to act."

After a short meeting with a social worker, of which Cheryl can't recall a single detail, she was led to the chapel, where she prayed for me. She had heard enough to understand that this wasn't about serious injuries or disabilities—this was about life or death.

As she was leaving the chapel to return to the SICU, she realized that someone from the hospital had been waiting for her. The young man in hospital scrubs quickly stood up, fell into step with her, and told her he would help her get back to me. For Cheryl, that was another reminder of the seriousness of the situation.

Before she arrived at my hospital, Cheryl and my other sister, Janice, had decided one of them should check on Kristi's status, so Janice and her husband, Joe Sauer, went to Scottsdale Memorial. Kristi repeatedly asked them about me, but they didn't have any reliable information either, so of course their vague answers reinforced Kristi's suspicion that I had been killed in the accident.

After having been assured that Kristi's injuries were not life threatening, they waited for her to fall asleep, and then Janice and Joe rushed over to County Hospital to check on me.

Evening turned to night at County, and the end of visiting hours approached with little change in my status. The medical staff then advised my sisters that a team from the nearby Barrows Neurological Institute was expected shortly to evaluate my condition and that there should be a status update available by midnight. So they settled in to wait. This proved to be the first of several long nights for them.

Shortly after midnight, a neurologist sat down with Cheryl and Janice. To help them understand the severity of my injuries, he explained to them that my brain, in its fragile envelope of water and soft tissue, had been forcefully driven up against my hard, bony skull. He advised them that there had been considerable swelling inside my brain, and the first 24 hours would be most critical. If I survived the first 24 hours, he said, the likelihood that I would survive would increase by a little bit—only a little bit. Then we would face the next 24 hours, and the next. In a nutshell (my pun, not the doctor's), it would be several days before the medical team would have confidence that I would live. To put it in the lexicon of sports; I was "day-to-day." Any conjecture regarding my degree of recovery or the possibility of permanent injury would have to wait at least until I had come through the early, critical days of recovering from swelling and bleeding in my brain.

The doctor then asked for permission to insert a brain shunt, if needed, to reduce swelling of my brain. The downside to this, he cautioned, was the possibility of additional brain damage. When my sisters asked what he would do if they did not grant permission, he stated that as a lifesaving measure, he would do it anyway. They signed the consent form, and the doctor urged them to go home and get some sleep. As it turned out, they didn't get much. At about 1:30 in the morning, the hospital called and told Janice my brain swelling had increased significantly and that they were going to insert the brain shunt. She quickly returned to the hospital.

The procedure took less than an hour, and after the shunt was inserted, my condition stabilized. Once again, I'd dodged a bullet.

ଚ

While there is never a good time to be notified that your son and daughter-in-law have been involved in a serious automobile accident, it proved to be a particularly challenging task to inform my parents.

From the time I was young, our family had vacationed in Rocky Point, Mexico, a small, sleepy town located near the north end of the Sea of Cortez, where shrimping was the primary industry. Rocky Point was just over 200 miles south of Phoenix, close enough for weekend jaunts to the beach. In fact, I spent a good deal of my youth there sailing, fishing, driving sand buggies, and trying to blow myself up with fireworks.

As time passed and the populations of Phoenix and Tucson exploded, Rocky Point began to grow into a huge vacation spot for the 'gringos.' There was no way this seaside paradise could be kept a secret for long.

On the day of our accident, my folks were staying at our family vacation spot about 20 miles down the coast from Rocky Point in a community called San Jorge. My brother Jim and his wife, Janice Kay, were with them. At that time, "our place" consisted of a motor home, a travel trailer, and a large gazebo. It was a bit primitive, quite far from Mexican civilization, and without piped-in water, electricity, or—even more importantly—telephone service. Communication to or from this part of the world was all but impossible.

After discovering that it was going to be very difficult to reach my parents, my friend Bob Schaefer swung into action. He had a connection in the Arizona governor's office. Through that connection he was able to contact the Mexican consulate, no small feat on a Saturday. The consulate staff was then able to get a message to the Mexican Red Cross in Rocky Point, which hand-delivered the message to my parents. By the time it finally reached them, though, it had been reduced to just a few words: the note said, "Steve Welker, bad accident." However, that was enough for my parents. Recognizing the effort it had taken to get this short note, my folks realized that the situation must truly be serious. They expeditiously packed and headed to Arizona.

Jim and Janice Kay had left Mexico before the Red Cross note arrived. They got back to Phoenix and received the bad news via multiple messages on their telephone answering machine. Without bothering to unpack their car, they headed for the hospital, grungy and sandy from their vacation, to check on my condition.

ᛦ

Sunday—day two—slowly passed with no major change in my condition. That evening, the medical staff came out and asked for two family members who could make decisions on my behalf. By this time, my parents had arrived, and the family decided that my Dad and my sister, Janice should meet with the staff.

The doctors had already warned my family that my brain injury could leave me with serious, permanent cognitive problems, meaning I would conceivably have to once again learn how to walk and talk.

The doctors were now trying to decide whether or not to perform a risky surgery that would alleviate the swelling of my brain. They felt that the surgery could quite possibly save my eyesight. On the other hand, they emphasized, it could also be fatal.

Should they or should they not do the surgery? This is the kind of question that no one can ever prepare for and that all of us hope we never have to answer.

The decision was narrowed down to two choices; either we could have the rest of our lives enjoying one another as family—sister, brother, husband, father and son—or lose me while hoping to save my sight.

I feel certain that their decision to forego the surgery saved my life. But, I have often thought, "What if that had been my decision?" I am so glad I was incapable of making the call. While I'm sure life and death decisions like this are made in hospitals several times a day, that fact does not make it any easier for those family members who are forced to make them. I am eternally grateful to my family who loves me enough to want me exactly as I am, not as they might have wished me to be.

A couple of years after the accident my Dad tearfully tried to apologize to me for making the decision that he thought had left me blind. I thanked him for making the courageous decision that allowed me to live.

On the same day my family made their fateful decision, Kristi's family arrived from Missouri to be with us. Her Dad and Mom, J.R. and Connie, and Kristi's sister Karla dropped everything and headed to Phoenix.

During those agonizingly stressful days, another critical decision was made regarding Kristi's left foot, which had been so badly damaged in the accident that most surgeons would have amputated it. Various important bones in her foot had been broken, and major nerves had been severed. Fortunately, a noted orthopedic surgeon was on call at the hospital, and after a detailed examination he elected to work to save her foot. Even though she still has some nerve problems and occasional pain—she is grateful.

Chapter 5

County Hospital

The first hospital I was taken to is a public facility operated by Maricopa County. Its patient population includes low-income and indigent patients and inmates of the state's penal system. The floor below the SICU was completely barred, and many of the patients/prisoners were handcuffed to their beds. As can well be imagined, the facility is not designed with all the conveniences of a modern hospital. The Mayo Clinic it is not.

The SICU, I am told, was functional at best. Most of the patient beds are located in a long, brightly lit clinical room that is divided down the middle by a large workstation at which nurses and doctors pore over charts, make phone calls and always look harried.

I was kept, virtually alone, in the very back portion of the room, where the lighting was subdued and the area was separated from most of the rest of the ward by the huge workstation. That isolated location, according to my family, was mute testimony to the fact that the staff didn't think I was going to survive. Several other patients who were nearby in the same section didn't live, and the word was that terminal patients were the only individuals who were privileged to reside in that zone.

During the next two days—days three and four—my condition improved somewhat. My family was counseled that, if I made it, I would probably have serious, lifelong physical and mental impairments. I wasn't talking at all during those first several days. And doctors said I would most likely suffer long-term head injuries, including memory loss and various other cognitive problems. In addition, they reported, I had already fallen heir to the usual hospital induced maladies of staphylococcus infection and viral pneumonia.

They also delivered the news that I was most likely blind. As a result of the intra-cranial swelling, my optic nerve had been damaged beyond repair. The doctors reluctantly showed Mom the brain scans that indicated my optic nerve was dead. This, they advised, would leave me totally, permanently blind. A conclusive diagnosis could not be made for a couple of days, they said, but based on their medical reports, blindness would be inevitable. My mom was left with the horrible task of telling the family. As she remembers that day, she says it was especially difficult because she did not yet believe it herself.

While I seemed to be turning the corner with respect to survival—no doubt a source of relief to everyone—I am sure their thoughts were: "At what cost? What will the quality of his life be? How will he be able to function as a father? A husband? A person?"

A few more days passed and I continued to improve, and suddenly, to the staff's complete amazement, I began to speak. I wasn't eloquent, but my cognitive ability was returning: I was talking. I'm told that I was disoriented and confused, having no idea where I was: often thinking I was at home, in the office, or at a store. Most of the time, I thought I was on the basketball court shooting hoops.

During one visit, I tried to convince Kristi that I had read in the newspaper that the hospital was manufacturing coffins in the basement so they could increase their revenue. She tells me that, in her fragile mental condition, she almost believed me.

I later learned that my disorientation was a result of both the head injury and the morphine drip that was being administered to manage my pain.

My family tells me that I quickly won the hearts of the hospital staff. Apparently, in cases of severe head injury; it is quite common for the patient to become angry and violent. Many of the patients in the SICU were literally chained to their beds. I, on the other hand, became known as the friendly basketball player. It is interesting for me to reflect on how "core" personality characteristics seem to come to the surface in traumatic situations. God has blessed me with a calm demeanor, and that is how I responded to this tragedy.

There was one nurse in particular who took my care very seriously. Unfortunately, no one can remember her name, but her memory is imprinted on my brain as simply "the red-haired nurse." My mom calls her my guardian angel.

The SICU had no waiting room. There were a couple of utilitarian, yellow-plastic chairs in the hallway outside the main door. Because God blessed me with an incredible family and devoted friends, there was never enough seating for everyone. Each morning, my buddies or family members would raid a nearby classroom for an extra dozen or so of the humble yellow chairs and would line them up just outside the SICU door. Each evening, the janitor would return them to the classroom. The yellow chairs took on a life of their own for my bevy of supporters. "Meet you at the yellow chairs" became a popular phrase.

The SICU visiting policy was strict. Only two or three immediate family members could visit me each hour, and a visit could last for only 15 minutes. Soon after the accident, three of my close buddies, anxiously waited outside the SICU every waking moment and were determined to see me, rules or no rules.

My mom felt sorry for them and decided to allow them to use one of her visitation times. She told them how to get back to the darkened side of the unit and instructed them to walk directly there. Mom says they came out of the unit shaken but much relieved from having actually seen me alive.

Unfortunately, this little transgression did not go unnoticed. My mom was sternly chastised by both my sister Janice and the red haired nurse. Mom decided that, given the situation, it was better to ask for forgiveness than permission. From that point on, my friends became "brothers-in-law" so they could gain occasional access to the SICU.

As fate would have it, the episode of the Leeza Gibbons show we had taped a couple of months earlier was broadcast two days after the accident. As Kristi and I lay in our respective hospital beds—with her panicked and in pain, and me quite literally clinging to life—our friends and family watched us excitedly sharing the story of our miracle babies.

In another corridor on the same floor of my hospital, my buddies furnished a small, TV-equipped waiting room with the same yellow chairs they were "requisitioning" from the classroom, and family and friends crowded in to see the broadcast. Due to a shortage of seating space, though, my friends gave up their seats to the ladies in my family and watched the show from the hall. The event was emotional and draining for everyone, including my strong, macho friends, and the hallway perch served well to conceal their tears. The guys would peer in for a few minutes until their emotions would catch up with them. Then they would step away from the doorway for a moment to gain their composure. The women, conversely, needed to cry and didn't care who saw them.

ဆ

During my stay at County, I was heavily sedated. Because I was semi-comatose, my friends and family members were anxiously attempting to get me to respond.

My friend Bob Schaefer took a cassette recorder to Kristi's hospital room so she could record some words of encouragement and love. While listening to the recording of her familiar, comforting voice, I am told I fervently kicked my feet and from that moment on I fought harder than ever to live.

On day ten, Kristi was released from Scottsdale Memorial Hospital. Doctors advised her to go straight home, but she insisted that her parents take her to see me. She was in a wheelchair, and her left foot was in a bulky cast. She was wearing a harness due to her broken collarbones. She had lost a lot of weight and was pitifully weak and gaunt. She was also suffering from serious closed head injuries—a fact that no one yet fully comprehended. After she reached my bedside, she asked to be left alone with me. She somehow managed to climb into my bed. What a sight it must have been to see two broken people huddled together in a hospital bed. How she managed to get onto that big bed—in her condition and with all those tubes and wires attached to me—one can only imagine. (I'm certain that the red haired nurse did not approve).

All told, I spent 12 *long* days in Maricopa County Hospital. By the Grace of God, I believe that in that dreary, frightening SICU I experienced a miracle. I believe that He wrapped his arms around me and allowed me to live. Apparently, I had some work left to do on this Earth.

Chapter 6

Facial Reconstruction Surgery

O n May 12th, twelve days after the accident, I had the first experience that I can clearly remember since that morning of April 30th. I was loaded into an ambulance—an ambulance that was transporting me from Maricopa County Hospital to St. Joseph's Hospital in Phoenix. I recall thinking that I was in no state of mind to really question where I was or what was happening. I'm not certain that I was even aware of my blindness. Of course, my head trauma and the painkillers dulled my thinking so that nothing was clearly registering.

It's a bit strange, that memory. Whenever I think about it I recall that in that moment I hadn't a thought about the accident itself, what had transpired in between, or how I had gotten into the ambulance, but—strangely—none of that alarmed me. All I knew for sure was, for some reason, I was helpless. I also knew that Kristi was there, and I was comforted that she was taking care of me.

During my time at County Hospital, Kristi had somehow managed to create the drive and determination to make some very important decisions regarding my care, despite the fact that she had spent ten days in the hospital, seriously injured and thoroughly battered. Still immobilized, in constant pain and under mild sedation, she spent hours on the phone trying to figure out the best possible course for my care.

At the same time, of course, she was breathlessly and ceaselessly monitoring Terri's precarious condition and the imminent premature birth of our twins.

Early on, Kristi had decided to move me away from Maricopa County Hospital as soon as possible. Her job with Bristol-Myers Squibb had taught her that County was a resident's hospital, a teaching hospital that was understaffed, overcrowded and under-funded. She had been calling on doctors' offices and hospitals for quite a while, and she knew from experience that the most seasoned doctors would not typically be found at County.

Having been updated on my medical condition, Kristi knew that my most important doctor, at least initially, would be my reconstructive surgeon. When she learned that the doctors at County were considering facial surgery but hadn't even asked to see a prior photo of me, her mind was made up. Kristi spent hours calling her contacts: physicians, co-workers, and friends, anyone she could think of who might know how to get me the best possible care. She was referred to the offices of Beals, Joganic and Holcombe. Dr. Beals met Kristi at the hospital and he reviewed my chart. He explained that he was going to be out of the Country. So, he referred my case to Dr. Travis Holcombe. Dr. Holcombe agreed to assume medical responsibility for my care, and his first instruction was to have me transferred to Barrows Neurological Institute at St. Joseph's Hospital. Neither Kristi nor I knew it at the time, but Dr. Holcombe's decision was a difficult one. There were risks involved, but he felt that they were worth taking. I am forever indebted to him.

Even though it is rare for a patient in critical condition to be transferred to another hospital, it turned out to be exactly the right move. I arrived in a better equipped medical facility, thus allowing evaluation and a surgical plan to emerge much sooner than if I had languished at County until I was medically strong enough to be moved. The staff at County did not agree with Kristi's decision or Dr. Holcombe's order to move me. They feared I would not survive the transfer.

While I give all of the credit in the world to Kristi for finding Dr. Holcombe, I believe that God put them together. Over the course of many surgeries. I've had since those frightening early days, Dr. Holcombe has become a mentor and a friend. More importantly, he has played an important role in my Christian walk.

My memories of the period immediately following my transfer to St. Joseph's are spotty, but I was aware even then that I was improving with each passing day. As soon as I stabilized from the transfer, we (well, the doctors) began planning the surgeries that would rebuild my face and hopefully save my right eye.

Dr. Holcombe brought in Dr. Peter Aiello to do the eye surgery. The first operation was scheduled for 9:00 p.m. on the 19th and would last for more than nine hours. As much as she wanted to be there with me, Kristi's medical problems prevented that.

Prior to the surgery, I was held in the prep room, already under mild sedation. Janice was with me, and I thank her for that. But I did make it tough for her. I was so thirsty! Time after time I would ask for water and she would tell me the instructions were to have *nothing* in my stomach prior to surgery. All she could do was hand me one of those little, flavor-impregnated wooden sticks given to patients who can't have anything to eat. No fluid, no nourishment, just flavor, hardly better than nothing, as far as I was concerned. I was weak and disoriented, but I kept trying to convince her that just a few drops of water would be OK. I remember thinking, "She's my little sister. I should be able to tell her what to do." Sometime during my discussion with her (she still calls it "begging") I drifted off into sleep.

The next thing I remember is waking up in the recovery room. I know that bad memories tend to fade over time, and thankfully I recall little of the pain except for the steel wires that were wrapped around my teeth and cutting into my mouth. My physician tells me that the nine-hour surgery was the longest, most complicated surgery he had ever performed.

Here are a few details of the operation. I relate them not to horrify you; rather, just to give you an idea of how miraculous it is.

In order to gain access to my facial structure, Dr. Holcombe first made an incision over the top of my scalp from ear to ear, thus allowing him to literally peel the skin of my face from the underlying muscles and bones so he and his assistants could work on the upper portion of my face.

The first task was to rebuild my nose. The accident had completely destroyed my nose cartilage. To replace the mutilated cartilage, the surgeon carefully carved out a scoop of my skull bone—from the right side of my head—and shaped it to replicate my nose cartilage, securing it to my facial bones with titanium plates and screws.

Then he made an incision in my mouth above the gums and inner upper lip, giving them access to my upper palate and nose.

Next, my cheekbones and forehead, which had also been crushed in the accident, were rebuilt and anchored in place with titanium plates and secured with screws.

And finally, the lower portion of my right orbital bone—the one that surrounds the eye—was rebuilt in the same fashion. In all, 19 titanium plates were fastened to my skull.

The right side of my face had taken the brunt of the impact, and the bones, eyelid and skin around my right eye had sustained the most damage. My right eye had been badly injured in the accident, and the doctors were not sure if they could save it—but that decision was for another time.

After the initial surgery was completed, the inside of my mouth was stitched closed, as was the long incision across the top of my head. Staples were inserted, as well, every inch or so along the skull incision. Capping things off, a metal support plate was attached to the bridge of my nose.

Even in the mind-fog of the recovery room, I remember thinking that, like Humpty Dumpty, all of this work might put me back together again.

Chapter 7

The Birth of Our Boys

On the day of the accident, Terri and J. J. were waiting excitedly at the Phoenix airport for Kristi and me. When we didn't arrive at the scheduled time, they began to get nervous. Then, when they heard their names over the paging system, they knew something was dreadfully wrong.

As Kristi was being transported to the hospital, she managed to convey to the paramedics that we had been on our way to the airport to meet our surrogate. Even though they didn't fully comprehend the ramifications of the situation, they were able to contact airport personnel to have Terri paged with the bad news.

Immediately after hearing the news, Terri and J.J. headed to Scottsdale Memorial Hospital to check on Kristi. They had been told that I probably wouldn't survive the accident. They wanted to stay in Phoenix to be with us, but Kristi, even in her injured state, was able to express to them the importance of going on to California for the impending birth of our boys. Reluctantly, they returned home so J. J. could pack a bag to go with Terri to California the next day.

On May 14, 1994, two weeks after our accident, as Kristi and I lay recovering, God blessed us with the birth of our boys, Colton and Dylan. They were both healthy, even though they were born nearly six and one half weeks prematurely. Because Terri had taken wonderful care of herself and followed doctor's orders to the letter, the boys were amazingly well developed, even statistically big for 33-week-old preemies.

At that time and in my fragile medical state, I barely knew who I was, and on the day of their birth I simply couldn't register that I had just become a father of twin boys. In fact, I still have no memory of it. My sister Janice tells me that she did, indeed, bring me the news and that I was happy to hear it, but it seemed to her that in just a few seconds I had forgotten all about this milestone event. At any rate, it certainly was not the kind of day I had planned for.

Because of their good health, the twins were released after only one week in the hospital. Truth is, Dylan could have come home earlier, but Colton was somewhat deprived of oxygen during the birth, so he needed to stay longer for observation, and Dylan hung in there as good company for his brother. After all, they'd been together for seven and one-half months, so what were a few more days?

Chapter 8

Recovery at
St. Joseph's Hospital

During the five weeks I spent in St. Joseph's Hospital, where I started my rehabilitation and recovery, I became very dependent upon my mother. In fact, I don't think I could have survived the mental or physical ordeal without her support, assistance and love.

At 37 years of age, I was 20 years past the time when most men "need" their moms. But this was an extraordinary situation, and I have an extraordinary mother. During this devastating period in my life, it was she who dropped everything to care for me.

It was very difficult for Kristi to get to the hospital, let alone to take care of me. She was still in a wheelchair, had her foot in a cast, and her mending collarbones were being protected by a harness that restricted her use of both arms. On top of all that, she had two 'preemie' babies at home to take care of. To see me, she had to enlist the help of two people—one to watch our babies and another to take her and her wheelchair to the hospital.

Enter Mom. Recognizing our situation, my mother swung into action with a vengeance. She moved from her home in Ajo, Arizona and into a hotel in Phoenix, just a few blocks from the hospital, where she stayed until the day I was released.

Throughout my recovery, eating was a painful process. Due to the damage to my mouth, both from the accident and from the surgery, and given that my teeth were wired together and covered with wax, there was no way I could eat solid food. Everything had to be soft or blended, deliverable through a straw! This mushy diet, combined with the trauma from the accident, produced a 35-pound weight loss—I was down to 140 pounds by then rather than my usual 175-pound 'fighting weight'. Whenever I stood up and revealed my six-foot three-inch height, I'm sure I looked like a skeleton with skin.

My mother quickly grasped the situation and realized how important my nutritional program was. She came to the hospital at least three times every day to feed me breakfast, lunch and dinner. I was tired, hurt and depressed most of the time with virtually no appetite. I honestly believe that if it hadn't been for my mom, I wouldn't have eaten at all.

My sleep patterns were much disrupted, too. I would wake up every morning at 3 or 4 a.m. Around 6, I would hear the reassuring sound of my mom's sandals coming down the hall. I remember so well that feeling of comfort welling up inside me by simply hearing the mundane sound of her sandals flip-flopping on the shiny, waxed hospital floor.

A few seconds later I would hear my mom's familiar, loving voice asking me if I was awake. I cannot explain the calmness and hope I felt from this simple inquiry.

The same amazing person who had been there throughout my childhood, my college years and my adulthood was once again there for me in my toughest hours. Yes, I know. She had never left. Although I could not see her (even when she was right there next to me) I knew she was there to take care of her son. I'll never know how I got lucky enough to be blessed with such an incredible mom.

As we spent those five weeks together, she showed absolutely no signs of pity for me. Nor did she ever express sadness about my disability. She was her usual, pleasant self, performing each task as if we were simply going through some everyday event. She never let on to me that this was tearing her up inside.

One morning, I didn't hear her footsteps at the usual time. I waited and waited, but she never came. Ever so slowly, an hour went by, and I became concerned that she wasn't going to show up. Was she all right? Where was she?

A few minutes after 7:00, she called and explained that she wasn't feeling well but would be in as soon as she felt better. What she did not tell me was that she was calling from another room in the same hospital—she had been admitted with gastrointestinal problems. I discovered this later, after my discharge, never having suspected what had really happened.

The ordeal of nearly losing her son and now witnessing him blind, lying in a hospital bed day after day, making slow progress at best—had taken its toll on her. The stress of the situation simply, finally, caught up with her.

During this downturn in her health she never let me know how serious her condition was. When I spoke with her on the phone, she sounded as upbeat as usual. Her main concern was still for me, regardless of her own status, and within a couple of days she was back to her regular visitation schedule. I don't remember eating anything during those few days she was away.

My mom was there for every major event during my hospital stay. Through all of the surgeries, the CAT scans, MRI scans, and the physical therapy sessions, she was there, making sure the doctors and nurses took care of her 37-year-old boy.

She also spent long hours just talking and comforting me. On one occasion, she decided I needed some sunshine—my mom is a big believer in the nutritional value of the sun's rays. Anyway, who was I to argue? I had nothing else to do. So she loaded me in a wheelchair and off we went to the hospital's outdoor patio. I was very nervous. This was the first time I had left my room for anything other than a medical procedure. How ridiculous it now seems that a grown man would be afraid to leave a hospital room—but that was the state of mind I was in. I didn't last very long on the patio. The sun seemed hot on that spring day in the desert, and I tired quickly, but I must admit that I felt better for having done it.

Sometime in the third week of my hospital stay, I began to walk.

The doctors at County, measuring my abilities with tests of my reflexes, had determined a couple of weeks earlier that I had the use of my legs. What they didn't and couldn't know, however, was to what degree my brain damage might impair my ability to walk. Would I be able to walk at all, or would I need to learn to walk all over again? Now that I was at St. Joseph's, and starting to gain some strength, it was time to find out.

For my first assessment, they wheeled me to a therapy room, with my sister Janice in tow. The staff was very nonchalant as they stood by and left Janice there to provide support for her fragile brother. She watched in pleasant shock as I casually stood up from the wheelchair and, using the rail attached to a wall, strolled off. Apparently, she was the only nervous person in the room; the staff continued to watch, unaffected.

Thereafter, I began taking short walks in the halls of the hospital with my mom and sister. I probably didn't actually travel much more than 50 feet in either direction, but these walks seemed like major ordeals to me—and were seen as major accomplishments by my family.

At first, walking down the halls in total darkness was completely overwhelming. Attempting such a simple task really brought home the impact that my disabilities had wreaked on my body. Often I would require a long nap to recover from even the shortest of our outings. My weakened physical state played a part, of course, but my fears also contributed a lot, too. But as difficult as it was for me, it was perhaps even more difficult for my family.

Mom has told me that the doctors had originally given the family a generally negative prognosis on every aspect of my recovery, so my family carried a heavy emotional burden from the beginning. On the other hand, as I accomplished each task—talking, walking, and so forth—even though I might have thought of it as nothing particularly special, the family greeted each event as a triumph. "We were so proud, each time," Mom says, "we saw what you were doing as courageous. We think it was actually *you* that brought *us* through it all."

The walks were very important to my healing process, but one day they almost came to an abrupt halt when, returning to my room at the end of a walk with my mom, I bumped my head on the bottom of the TV suspended from the ceiling. I stand a full foot taller than my mom, so she walked easily under the TV, but I didn't make it. Fortunately, I wasn't injured, but Mom was mortified—so much so that I had to beg her to take me on my walk the next day.

Even today, this height difference is a common problem whenever I am walking with a sighted guide who is shorter than me. Sometimes I even remind Mom that it happens with other people, too, because she still feels guilty about running me into that TV.

For Mom, taking care of me in the hospital was a major time commitment, one in which I will never be able to adequately thank her. I've tried. But she quickly dismisses my attempts at expressing gratitude, claiming that any mother would do the same for her son." I don't think so.

My mom is a very busy person, and I'm quite sure that she was greatly missed at work while she was tending to me. Most folks her age have retired, bought a motor home and toured all of the lower 48 states. Not her! Mom (and Dad) operate three insurance agencies and a convenience store—and those are just a few of their ventures.

As my stay at Barrows dragged on, with more and more tests, procedures, evaluations, assessments and surgeries, I became increasingly aware of how serious my situation was. Once, in the middle of the night, I called my sister Cheryl and told her she had to come get me out of the hospital right then. I had just awakened from a nightmare in which I thought I was being turned into a cauliflower. Whether from the morphine or the head injury, I'll never know but it was terrifying!

After one particularly bad night of morphine-induced nightmares, I told the nurse that I wanted the IV tube removed right then. I would rely on oral painkillers from that point on, thank you very much. I figured there was no way the pain could be as bad as the nightmares.

Over the next couple of days, as the residual narcotic effects of the morphine began wearing off, I slowly started to become more aware of my situation. But it wasn't a clear, complete picture in my mind. I was still on prescription drugs and had a major head injury, so the full impact of my blindness had not yet hit me.

It was a bit of a slippery slope, this withdrawal from the high-octane painkillers. My brain began to clear, and then, early one morning, I got the first real indication that I was seriously disabled. I attempted to complete the simple task of changing the station on the radio that was built into the hospital bed and couldn't do it! I remember the sinking feeling, the confusion and the awful realization that I was no longer 'competent' or 'complete'.

At about the same time, I felt a nagging, persistent pain in my right hand. An x-ray revealed that it was broken in two places. Apparently, the morphine and other medications had masked the pain. My hand was put in a cast, causing me to be even more incapacitated.

Another indicator revealing my limitations occurred after I had been at Barrows for a couple of weeks. A nurse came in and told me she needed to give me a shower. I convinced her that I was strong enough to do the task myself. After all, I was a grown man and I had been giving myself showers for over 30 years. (I am also a fairly modest guy and didn't want to go through the embarrassment of requiring help with this personal grooming chore.) Reluctantly, she consented. I remember going into the bathroom, removing my gown and getting into the shower. Suddenly I realized that I was very light headed. After all, I hadn't stood for any length of time on my own for several weeks. I then passed out. The next thing I remembered was hearing the high-pitched, urgent voices of the nursing staff around me as I lay crumpled on the floor.

I never again saw the nurse I'd sweet-talked into letting me shower alone. I felt guilty and really wanted to apologize to her. It was certainly no fault of hers; I have always had the ability (or maybe it is a disability) of being able to persuade people to embrace my point of view. I'm sure I came across as very believable when I told her that I was strong enough to shower myself.

After that incident, I was unwilling to shower at all, even with assistance, and I couldn't be talked into it. A week or two later, however, a nurse (someone at least as convincing as me) talked me into allowing her to give me a shower in a large enclosure. The facility was equipped with a chair, and I was a little stronger than I had been the first time. At any rate, it did feel good to be clean again.

The simple task of brushing my teeth was a major ordeal, too, because almost every tooth in my mouth was wrapped in wire and wax. To clean my teeth, a nurse had to remove the old wax, clean with a water pick, and then apply new wax. I couldn't use a toothbrush because of all the wire and wax, plus the fact that many of my teeth were very loose, a fragile state-of-the-mouth, indeed. All in all, dental hygiene was a painful, messy project. My teeth were sensitive and it hurt to have the wax removed and reapplied. And to cap it all off, the water pick sprayed water all over and was awkward to use. This was supposed to be done every day, but I balked, allowing a nurse to do it only every two or three days—cavities were the least of my worries!

My rehabilitation time in the hospital became a slow, draining process. Not long after my first major surgery, my neurologist, Dr. Kathryn Plenge, decided that I should begin working with a speech therapist, an occupational therapist and a physical therapist.

The speech therapist read long stories and asked me to recall and repeat pertinent facts. Sometimes she would ask me to repeat certain words—apparently a test of my memory skills. And to test my math skills she gave me increasingly complex problems to solve. I thought I was doing well at these tests. In reality, I was failing miserably. But just as muscles strengthen with exercise, my brain became stronger and sharper with these mental exercises.

The occupational therapist tested me for manual dexterity and problem solving skills. She placed small items such as bolts and coins into clay to determine if I could retrieve them. There was also a lot of square peg in the square hole stuff. I hated it—these tests were very challenging. Yes, I did need help in many areas. The good news was the therapists were pleasantly surprised at my progress.

The physical therapist brought large rubber bands to my room so I could work on strengthening my muscles. He also had me try to stand on one foot for extended periods of time. I'm sure it had something to do with balance, but even today I don't know why he had *me* do this when most *healthy* people can't even do it.

Eventually, I was taken to the workout area to ride an exercise bike, but I was so weak I would only last a minute or two.

The therapists, cumulatively, spent three hours with me each day, Monday through Friday. I dreaded the appointments because they drained me. I still found it hard to believe that these relatively brief and easy activities could be so tiring. After all, it had been only a month or so since I had played basketball three times a week in three-hour stints. But now, all I wanted to do was sleep.

I also met with a psychiatrist a couple of times. I don't remember much about these sessions, but one thing we discussed really stuck with me. "Prior to your accident," the psychiatrist asked, "what was the worst thing that ever happened to you?"

I had to think long and hard on that one. Looking back, I realized that I had led a pretty charmed life. I had never lost a member of my immediate family, nor had any of them ever been involved in a serious accident or suffered from a debilitating illness. My mom and dad had been married forever. I had never been laid off or fired from a job. I was addicted to nothing but caffeine and suffered from no personality disorders (that I knew of). I had never been divorced—and, best of all; I was happily married to the woman of my dreams!

"Well," he responded, "you have been very lucky. But, sadly, life is just not like that. Bad things happen in life. And you have been very fortunate to have made it this far with no major incidents."

Although I didn't feel very fortunate, I knew what he was telling me. Welcome to the real world.

⊱

My days at St. Josephs were filled with visits from family members and friends—lots and lots of friends. To be honest, I didn't know I had so many friends.

I have been told that visits to a sick or injured loved one can be harder on the visitor than the patient, and in retrospect I can understand why. Everyone who visited me attempted to put on a positive face while with me, but I'm sure their true emotions were much different.

As for me, I was just trying to muster the energy to get through each day. My mom was closely monitoring my visitors. I wanted to see everyone who came to the hospital, but she knew that I didn't have the stamina. She wouldn't let everyone in, but later she would tell me about their visits.

As it turned out, at the time of the accident my younger sister Janice was between jobs. This coincidence (if you believe there are such things) was a true Godsend for Kristi and me. Janice was often there with Kristi and the boys, helping out with anything from transportation to all-around support, and she was able to visit me in the hospital virtually every day.

One day when I was feeling particularly strong, alert and aware of my hunger, I developed a craving for a chocolate milkshake. As soon as Cheryl and Janice arrived for their afternoon visit, I insisted that they take me to the cafeteria so I could get one. Nervously, they loaded me into the wheelchair and away we went.

In recalling the event with my sisters, they tell me that they were both very concerned about taking me away from my hospital room and the nurse's station. They had no idea what they would do if I had a medical emergency.

Cheryl figured that Janice seemed to know what she was doing and decided to follow suit. Janice remembers being concerned about the situation, but my casual attitude put her at ease. As for me, I had a head injury, and I just wanted a chocolate milk shake. No big deal!

While we waited in the cafeteria line, I suddenly remembered that only a month earlier I had been in this very cafeteria—J.J. and I had come here on the night Terri had gone into pre-term labor. What a difference a month could make! One month earlier I had been worried about the fate of our unborn boys—now I was worried about my own fate!

After we got our milk shakes, we went out to the courtyard for a 'normal' conversation among three siblings. Cheryl remembers it as one of the first moments that she felt any reason for optimism for getting her brother back. I think that I, too, felt a little better after that family outing—a bit more normal, indeed. And slowly the progress continued.

In my room one day, as Dr. Holcombe and I were talking about my basketball prowess, he asked me, "Who are your favorite Phoenix Suns players?" Thinking that he was just making small talk, I told him I thought that Charles Barkley had made the biggest impact on the team and was the most popular, but Kevin Johnson (KJ) was probably my favorite player.

A year earlier, in 1993, the Suns had played the Chicago Bulls for the NBA championship. Barkley and Johnson were the keys to that successful run. Barkley was always good for a controversial quote, but Johnson seemed to be the one with the best attitude.

A few days after our conversation, Kristi came to my hospital room and asked me to get cleaned up and put on some clothes. Seeing no reason to waste my energy, I decided to stay in my hospital gown. What Kristi was keeping from me was that Dr. Holcombe was on his way with a friend.

A few minutes later, Dr. Holcombe walked in and introduced his companion, Kevin Johnson. We shook hands, and Kevin drew up a chair.

"How do I know you're really KJ?" I said, half jokingly, half seriously. "You could be anybody."

"You caught me!" he responded. "I'm actually the janitor. The staff asked me to come in here and tell you that I was KJ."

We had a nice conversation that day. The majority of it, as I recall, focused on my relationship with Kristi. KJ wasn't married, and he wanted to know how we'd met and how we had known we were in love. Left unasked, I'm sure, was: "Where can I get a woman like Kristi—one who would stick by my side if I went through this kind of tragedy?"

Dr. Holcombe then told me his 'secret'. He was one of the Phoenix Sun's team physicians and also the son-in-law of valley luminary Jerry Colangelo, CEO of the Suns.

KJ brought me a Suns jersey and a cap—not an unusual gesture for a sports star—but his interest in me didn't end that day. After I returned home from the hospital, he sent me personal notes and an inspirational book entitled *If You Could See What I Hear*. The author, Tom Sullivan, is blind and I could really relate to his challenges.

I greatly appreciated the personal interest that Kevin showed me during this tumultuous time. Over the years, I have kept in touch with him, directly and indirectly. In my opinion, he is a class act.

On other visits, Dr. Holcombe brought Gary Bender, the nationally recognized sports broadcaster. Once, when we had advance notice, we produced a 'full house'—several of my family members and a few of my sports-minded buddies—and Gary kept us entertained with stories of his dreams of being a sportscaster since he was a kid. He told us he would make up full-length baseball games and pretend to be the announcer while plowing the fields on his daddy's farm tractor.

During the meeting, Gary asked me if I would help him with his play by play. He wanted me to listen to some of his broadcasts and give him my critique. He thought that a blind person might be able to help provide a unique perspective on his play calling that a sighted person might miss. It was a thoughtful request.

Before one of my surgeries, Dr. Holcombe asked if it would be OK to have Gary join us in the prep area for a pre-surgery prayer. This laudable gesture meant a lot to me. The fact that this guy, who really didn't know me, cared enough to be there to provide support at this critical time really affected me. I hope those in the room that day didn't see the tears running down my face.

One night, after Mom had gone back to her hotel, a good friend, Stan Sipes, stopped by my room (sneaking in after visiting hours). As only Stan could, he pulled up a chair, kicked his feet up, and started talking to me as though nothing had happened. Stan is one of those guys who is everyone's 'best friend'—a very personable, likeable guy and the life of any party. He has a great sense of humor and the unique ability to put people at ease no matter the circumstances. After I felt him put his feet on my bed, he said, "So, Soft, how are you doing?"

Soft? Oh, I forgot to mention, Stan is also the king of nicknames. He has a nickname for everyone. He started calling me "Soft and Fragile." The occasion was my friend Dino Paul's bachelor party. I wouldn't drink shots of tequila with the guys, and Stan thought that was "soft." That was in 1990, and the name stuck. Lucky me!

Stan and I talked for a while, but I was tired and don't remember much of the conversation. As he got ready to go, he said, "You know, Soft, you should have listened to me and learned to go left."

When it occurred to me what he meant, I started laughing out loud for the first time since my accident. You see, Stan and I had played basketball together for many years, so we knew each other's game pretty well. Stan knew that when I had the ball, I would always drive to my right. Sometimes, Stan would get so frustrated with my deficit that he'd tell my opponents about it even when he wasn't playing. He would stand off-court at the baseline and scream at the guy covering me, "He can't go left! He can't go left!" Stan's comment in my hospital room that night was, of course, in reference to the fact that I had pulled off to the right side of the road just before the accident.

Another important visitor was a good friend, Brian Scott (or "names" as Stan nicknamed him because Brian has two first names). Brian and I have been friends since high school and have been through life's ups and downs together.

Brian and his wife, Jackie, were living in San Diego at the time. They were in town for the bachelor party/wedding of our mutual friend Jeff Pawlowski. Jackie was doing the wedding's floral arrangements.

After hearing about the accident, Brian drove straight to County hospital to check on me. He was told I probably wouldn't live through the night and his thoughts immediately went to Kristi.

The following day he and Jackie went to Scottsdale Memorial to check on Kristi's condition. From then until Kristi was released Brian spent a lot of time with her each and everyday. He still came by to check on me but correctly surmised that I was in no mental condition to be aware of his presence.

While Brian may not be the most sensitive and empathetic man in the world, his true character really rose to the occasion during these trying times. I will never forget his incredible support of my wife as she struggled with the reality of what lie ahead.

To this day, Brian shrugs off his continual support by saying he didn't have anything else to do. Don't worry; I don't buy that weak alibi for a minute. Kristi says of all of the visitors she had, it is Brian's confident reassurances that she most fondly remembers.

On Memorial Day, Dino Paul showed up with a radio so we could listen to the Indianapolis 500 race. I was a big Indy 500 fan and Dino knew it. I had even gone back to the brickyard in 1989 to watch the race in person. I don't recall Dino being an Indy fan or even bringing a TV so he could watch the race himself. As a matter of fact, I don't think Dino liked racing at all. What I do remember, however, is falling asleep for long stretches during the race and waking up each time with Dino there at my side to give me the status. True friends show their colors during the trying times.

Another important visitor was a guy I didn't even know but over the years has become both a good friend and a staunch supporter. Patrick

McGroder arrived early one evening, introduced himself and sat down, announcing that Kristi had retained him as our legal counsel.

My initial thought was, "Watch out!"

Having come from the insurance field, my only dealings with personal injury attorneys had been fairly negative. From what I had been able to determine, they were all a bunch of ambulance chasers whose only ambition was maximizing settlements in order to line their own pockets. (I was about to have that perception blown away.)

As incapacitated as my brain was, I began grilling Pat on his fee structure. He patiently answered all of my questions in great detail, even though I probably didn't "get it." In spite of the fact that Kristi had already retained him, I think Pat was trying to make me feel important. It was obvious that I was in no condition to make any decisions.

That visit spoke volumes about Pat's character. Not only was I mentally incapacitated, but I also had absolutely no memory of the accident. He knew he couldn't get 'facts' about the event from me. The real reasons he came by were to get to know me and see how I was coping.

In retrospect, I think that Pat may have been a bit shaken by our meeting. On many occasions since, he has commented that we look so much alike, we could be brothers. We are almost exactly the same size, 6'3" tall and about 175 pounds, with similar hair, face and bone structure. I suspect he might have been thinking, "The man lying in this hospital bed could be me."

As we talked, I began to let my guard down, and we started having an easy-going, casual conversation. All of a sudden, out of nowhere, an odd thought clicked in my brain, and out of the clear blue I asked Pat if he owned a collection of American muscle cars that he stored in a warehouse. If I could have seen him, I'm quite sure I would have watched his jaw drop in astonishment.

How did I know this? And more importantly (to me), how did I manage to remember it when nearly everything else in my past was foggy at best? Well, nearly ten years earlier, while I was working at Westfield Insurance, we had written a policy on his warehouse and I had inspected the property. I'd been very impressed with his collection.

To say it was amazing that such obscure facts would come to me in my fragile mental state would be a serious understatement. And that Pat had been guided to my bedside was more than mere coincidence.

Before Pat left, he reached out and gave me a hug. With thick emotion in his voice, he told me everything was going to be OK and he was going to take care of us. Little did I know at that time that he was truly a man of his word. Today, over a decade after our accident, both Kristi and I value him as a good friend and advocate. And I have also learned an important lesson: Judge people by their character, not their profession.

Chapter 9

New Dad

I t wasn't until the third week of May that I had my first memory of—and feelings about—being a new father. I had discussions about the boys' birth with Kristi, my mom and my sisters, but until that day, it had never really impacted me. On May 21st, Terri and J.J. arrived in Phoenix with our sons, now just seven days old. They met Kristi and me at the hospital so they could bring us our tiny miracle babies.

The staff set up a special room for us, then a nurse wheeled me in. One at a time, our tiny little guys were handed to me to hold. I will never forget the first time I held my boys to my chest. That very day I gave Dylan a nickname that we still call him today: Big Dog. Not that he was any more important to me than Colton; it was just that he was, and still is, bigger than his twin brother.

I remember holding Colton and thinking that he was a tiny little guy. Because of his premature birth he weighed only four pounds, two ounces.

I must admit, the memorable significance of this moment didn't fully register in my brain. I was in such a confused state; I knew these were my babies, but I had too many other things to worry about, and no matter how hard I tried to remain alert, I tired after only a few minutes and had to ask to be taken back to my room so I could rest.

They won't admit it to me, of course, but I'm sure that Kristi, Terri and J.J. all must have wondered, as I was wheeled from the room, "What kind of a father will this man be? He spent only a few minutes with his new babies. Will he ever be able to fully understand that these boys are his? Have we made a mistake bringing them into this world? Would he have been better off if he had died in the accident?"

For the rest of my hospital stay, Kristi visited me as often as she could, but due to the constraints of her wheelchair and the enormous logistics of transporting herself and the babies and all their paraphernalia, she could bring only one of our sons at a time. She would have someone put whichever one she had brought that day on my chest, to let me hold and talk to him. To this day, Kristi still questions whether I really understood that these were our sons. My recollection is that I did, but I really can't be sure. I do, however, remember the feelings of love that enveloped me in those moments, both for the boy-of-the-day and for my wife.

During her visits, I would ask Kristi to come lie with me on the bed— she says I made this request every time she visited, sometimes more than once. Or I would ask her to help me get to the bathroom. She would try to explain to me she couldn't do these things because she was in a wheelchair. I just didn't seem to grasp that what I was asking of her was nearly impossible. These were very difficult times for Kristi, painful reminders of how much I struggled cognitively. She must have been devastated seeing the husband she had known only as a healthy, active man now reduced to this shell of his former self.

Part Three:
"Thy rod and thy staff, they comfort me . . ."

Chapter 10

Release from the Hospital

After spending three full weeks in Barrows undergoing daily therapy treatments and allowing my body to continue to heal, the medical staff approved a weekend visit home. The therapy sessions were scheduled only on weekdays and there wasn't much going on over the weekends.

The fact that my body was up for the visit didn't mean my mind was. When given the opportunity to go, I initially declined. By this time, I didn't think I could survive outside the hospital. I believed all that was keeping me alive were the doctors and nurses and the medical equipment. I worried that if I left this safe microcosm, my fragile body wouldn't be able to survive the outside world.

As the weekend drew near, Kristi was somehow able to allay my fears, and I agreed to go home for one night. As my sister Janice drove Kristi to the hospital Saturday morning to pick me up, I became more and more nervous. The hospital was, after all, the only home I had known since the accident.

I'm sure Kristi was nervous, too, but she didn't show it. I must have appeared so fragile when she arrived that morning. My face was still bruised from the injuries and surgeries, my teeth were wired together, I was down 35 pounds and I had taken only one shower over the last five weeks. And, oh, yes, I almost forgot, I was now blind.

If I ever need to remember what true, unconditional love looks like, I need look no further than this amazing woman. Loving someone when times are good is easy. The true test of love comes during the tough times, and these certainly qualified.

I was wheeled into the parking lot by what seemed to be the entire staff at Barrows. I was immediately greeted by the reality of the hot summer in the desert; the intense heat hit me full force. I again began to question the wisdom of leaving the safety and comfort of the hospital.

As we traveled home, it didn't seem real to me. Janice was driving and Kristi sat next to me in the back, comforting me. I could feel we were on the freeway, but I could see nothing. This real world, I feared, was going to be scary.

After we pulled into our driveway, I was bombarded with intense emotion. As I walked to my door, I couldn't believe how strange it felt. I was walking on the sidewalk in my front yard, past all of the landscaping I had planted myself, but now I couldn't see it. My yard, which I had seen a thousand times, was now just blackness to me.

As Janice opened the front door, I was greeted by a pleasant surprise. An exuberant Lucy, our Pomeranian, excitedly ran circles around me and jumped at my legs. I had completely forgotten about her during the past five weeks in the hospital, and this warm homecoming brought a much needed smile to my face.

For some reason I can't explain, Lucy had always favored me. It didn't bother Kristi and she joked that Lucy was my dog. During my absence, Kristi told me, Lucy had worried herself sick. She wouldn't eat and she'd lost a lot of weight. She had spent most of her time grieving under my side of the bed.

Some people claim dogs have a special sense and know when bad things have happened. Judging from how excited Lucy was to see me, it's hard to disagree.

After entering the house, I immediately headed for the family room couch. I was already tired and needed to rest. As I sat there, I began to feel the familiar couch with my hands. Although I couldn't see it, I was comforted by the fact that I knew exactly what it looked like. I knew the colors and patterns. Even though I was in my home, however, it wasn't the same home I had left on April 30th.

The first thing that was apparent was the number of people. Kristi's mom was there to help. There was another friend staying with her—Linda Mack, from Oregon, who had mentored Kristi during the surrogacy. In addition, a couple of neighbors were there to greet me.

The biggest change was the distinct sound of babies rocking back and forth in their swings. They were cooing to each other and seemed very unimpressed by their daddy's triumphant return. Kristi brought them to me one at a time so I could start to get to know my boys.

I didn't last long on the couch. The whole ordeal of coming home had exhausted me, and I told Kristi I needed to take a nap. She helped me find my way to our room, to our familiar bed, where I quickly fell asleep.

When I awoke a couple of hours later, I didn't know where I was. I knew it was too quiet to be my hospital room. Without the benefit of sight, I couldn't immediately identify my surroundings.

After hearing Kristi's rhythmic breathing next to me as she slept, I remembered where I was. I lay there quietly, listening to her breathe, worried that the familiar, reassuring sound would stop. This proved to be the first of many times I would do this for long stretches in the middle of the night. I was terrified that this wonderful person taking care of me would die.

Another interesting phenomenon developed during this time. Whenever I pictured Kristi in my minds eye, I saw her with a halo over her head. I'm sure now that I was seeing her as my own personal angel. I think I was seeing something that's as real as can be, but is invisible to the naked eye.

After we woke up from our nap, Kristi gently suggested I let her give me a bath. I must have been comfortable with my own wife giving me a bath because I agreed.

As she tells it now, it was much more difficult than she let on. To see the emaciated, bruised body of her formerly healthy husband was almost more than she could bear. She was up to the task of being my personal angel, though, and she thoroughly bathed me and shampooed my filthy hair.

Later, as we sat in the family room with our babies, I felt more alive than I had since the accident. I decided right then and there that I wanted to come home for good, as soon as possible. This was my home, my wife, and my boys, and this was where I belonged.

The following day I went back to the hospital. There wasn't much activity at Barrows on that Sunday afternoon, and for the very first time,

I felt I didn't belong there. I had an overwhelming feeling I should be at my home with my wife and kids, regardless of my physical condition.

The next week in the hospital was a long one. I plodded through all of my therapy sessions, but my mind was on the return home. I was nervous but cautiously eager to get started with my new life, whatever that was going to look like.

Before I could be released from the hospital, all of my various doctors and therapists had to sign off on my discharge. The exit interview was scheduled for Saturday morning. They would all be in attendance: my doctors, therapists, my parents, and Kristi.

Wanting to look my best, I took a shower on Friday morning. I decided that I also needed to shave. I had not done so in seven weeks. It was obvious I couldn't shave myself, so I agreed to allow a male nurse to shave me. I rationalized that he could do a better job than a female nurse as he had more experience.

Motionless and deep in thought, I sat in the bathroom while he lathered my face with the cream. As he began shaving my face, a dark feeling of helplessness overtook me. I thought, "Is this what my life is now reduced to? Am I going to have to rely on others from now on?"

Like a ton of bricks, it hit me. This might be the way things are going to be from now on. I am blind and, short of a miracle, will be for the rest of my life. For the first time, I plunged into a deep trough of pity. Quietly, I began to cry. I'm sure the nurse saw this, but he thankfully didn't say anything.

On Saturday morning, I was led down to a conference room for the meeting. I felt like I was going before a parole board. During the meeting, I tried to act as "normal" as I could, because I didn't want to spend another night in that hospital.

Looking back on it, I think the treatment team had already agreed to let me go home. The meeting turned out to be more about my continued care than anything else, and I was immediately released.

Linda Mack was with Kristi to drive us home. I was still nervous, but excited. Finally, I was going home for good!

This meant that my mom was "released," too. This incredible woman, who for the last two months had been with her son every day, could now go home to sleep in her own bed. I'm sure it was a great relief to her. I didn't realize it then, but her time tending to me probably aged her ten years.

ʬ

Even after I returned home, I was faced with an unending barrage of doctor appointments. On some days, I would have two (or even three) of them. There were visits to the hand doctor to have pins removed and to get physical therapy, trips to the cardiologist to monitor my heart, appointments with my general practitioner to tend to bed sores on my head, and meetings at the neurologists to check my healing progress and emotional state.

I was also seeing my ophthalmologist every week. He was vigilantly checking for vision in my left eye, regularly testing with a strong light to determine pupil dilation and to detect any light perception that I might have retained.

After one such appointment, he determined that I could see some minor contrast between light and dark. It was so minor that I hadn't even noticed it myself.

At the end of the visit, he made a very strange comment. He told me that just because a blow to my head had caused my blindness, another blow would not give it back. Who did he think I was, Elmer Fudd?

Shortly after I got home from the hospital, I developed a toothache in a wisdom tooth. The pain became so intense, I had to put a rubber block between my teeth to keep me from biting down on it.

A visit to my dentist revealed that the tooth was cracked in half, probably as a result of the accident. Because the upper plate had been disturbed, my bite was now crooked and my teeth were incorrectly aligned. I also learned that, because I was finally off of strong painkillers, I could feel the pain full force!

I was referred to a specialist for the necessary extraction. Due to the amount of anesthesia I had recently been given, the dentist was not comfortable putting me under. So, after three hours and enough numbing medication to paralyze an elephant, he finally pulled the tooth. The relief from the incredible pain was immediate.

A week or so after that, it was time to have the metal wires removed from my teeth. I was really looking forward to this, as it would allow me to start eating normal food and to brush my teeth, something I had not done in nearly two months. It would also mark an end to the painful task of cleaning my teeth and wires.

As it turned out, this proved to be a very painful experience. I received no anesthesia to deaden the pain, and the wire was pulled out from between my teeth with pliers. Although the procedure took only a few minutes, it remains in my memory as one of the most painful parts of my entire ordeal.

Probably as a result of the pain and my depressed emotional state, I simply 'lost it' as my sister Janice drove Kristi and me back home. The thought of what a dark swamp my life had become, plus the seemingly bleak future I had to look forward to, hit me all at once.

Quietly crying, I felt ashamed that Janice and Kristi would see me in this state, but I just couldn't help it. The trip was somber and silent. I think they instinctively knew that they needed to leave me to my thoughts. It was a heartbreaking moment for all of us.

In September of 1994, three months after my hospital discharge, I had an important—and emotional—decision that I needed to make regarding my severely damaged right eye.

Blood flow to the eye had become restricted, and the damage to the muscles was not healing. As a result, the eyeball was, in effect, dying, slowly shrinking in size, and would eventually shrivel up. After several meetings with the eye surgeon, I made the tough decision to have it removed.

During the surgery, the doctor would also have to insert plastic tubes to replace my tear ducts, which had also been destroyed and could no longer provide proper drainage.

After the surgeon removed the eye, he inserted a round piece of polished coral into the eye socket. Coral is used in these procedures because its porous nature allows the muscle strands to attach to the substitute eyeball. This procedure was elected in the hope that I would still have some movement available for a future prosthetic eye.

Unfortunately, the muscles were too badly damaged, and I have never been able to regain any movement.

The surgery seemed to go well, but complications set in after we returned home. During the surgery, cartilage was taken from behind my right ear and used to help rebuild my orbital socket. The painful incision behind my ear continued to bleed, and the flow couldn't be stopped. Therefore, we had to return to the hospital so my head could be re-bandaged. At the same time, the surgeon inserted a tiny tube into the injured area so Kristi could inject painkiller directly.

Unfortunately, the procedure didn't stop the bleeding, so early the next morning we had to once again go back to the hospital. This time, the doctor decided to cauterize the area. As I had been anesthetized for so long during the original surgery, they elected not to use a general anesthesia, so the procedure was done with a local. I had the pleasure of lying there, fully awake, while they burned the incision behind my ear to close it properly.

In February of 1995, I was back for more surgery with Dr. Holcombe on the same general area. He removed more cartilage from behind my ear, and fatty tissue was removed from my abdomen to help rebuild my right orbital socket. This was not a major surgery, but each return to the hospital set me back emotionally, reminding me of what I had already been through. My lesson from this? I learned that a "minor" surgery to a doctor is not a 'minor' surgery for the patient.

After my eye socket and lid had healed from all of the surgeries, it was time for a trip to the ocularist. Never heard of an ocularist? Don't worry, neither had I. An ocularist is a special craftsman who makes prosthetic eyes, commonly called 'glass eyes.' This term, however, is inaccurate. They are neither glass—nor are they round. They are actually made of acrylic and shaped like an extra large contact lens.

An ocularist is really more of an artist than a technician, in my opinion, and the fabrication and fitting processes require a real talent. After the acrylic mold is custom-fitted to the eye socket, the ocularist goes to work at his craft, painting the lens not only to look realistic but also to match perfectly the existing eye for color, pupil size and blood vessels.

Objectively speaking, this isn't a topic I ever thought I would be the least bit interested in, much less telling others about. Like so many things in life, though, most of us seem to have an incredible ability to accept things that aren't 'normal'.

When I was first wearing the prosthesis, Kristi had to help me with the occasional removal and cleaning. She was a real trooper about it, dutifully performing the delicate chore whenever it was required, even though it was certainly not something she had signed up for when she married me.

This routine maintenance chore, it turned out, was often a time when the sadness that underlies long-term disabilities would hit us full force. But sometimes, one of these occasions would provide a welcome signal of great emotional progress for one or the other of us—or both of us. During one session in particular, we realized that we were becoming emotionally stronger. Kristi had just cleaned the prosthesis in the bathroom sink and had reached out to pick up a towel with which to dry it. In our bathroom, the towel rack hung directly over the toilet and, you guessed it, she accidentally dropped the eye into the toilet! I was lying just a few feet away from the bathroom door, on our bed, and I distinctly heard the "ker-plunk" as it hit the water, followed immediately by the swishing sound of her hand diving into the reservoir to recover the fugitive orb. Instantly, I knew what had happened. I held my breath. After a brief moment—which could have triggered embarrassment and demoralization—she began to laugh, rather quietly and hesitantly at first, but then louder and more freely. Before I knew it, I was laughing, too, and moments later we were rolling around on our bed, laughing not only at ourselves but also at how incredibly complex—and sometimes silly—our lives had become.

Chapter 11

Depression Sets In

As the days and nights passed and I became increasingly aware of my situation, I was regularly hit with waves of massive depression. It was almost unbearable to think that I was completely blind and probably would be for the rest of my life.

In the initial stages of my recovery, I believe that my head injury and all those painkilling drugs prevented me from completely understanding the full ramifications of this total, permanent disability. Now, without any "miracle cure" on the horizon, I resigned myself to the fact that the wonderful life I had once had was dead and gone.

It wasn't unusual for me to break down many times each day. I came to treat it as a minor success when I could go for an entire hour without simply 'losing it.' Just about anything and everything that reminded me of my blindness could bring on sadness, even tears.

The first weeks at home were surreal, to say the least. It was as though I was living in a bad dream; but I knew it was not a dream. Some things, like my house, my furnishings and my wife were very familiar to me. But many other things, mainly living in the dark, were not. What had happened to my life?

Every action seemed to add to the burden I had to carry. For instance, it was incredibly depressing and frustrating to stumble around my home. I had a difficult time finding my way from the bedroom to the kitchen in a house in which I had lived for six years. Our home, a floor plan I had navigated so easily just a couple of months before, was now a confusing, black maze to me!

To further complicate matters, there were now many new obstacles in my path. With the babies came all of the equipment they required. This included baby swings, playpens, cribs and rocking chairs; all of which were frequently moved. In addition, we had a couple of extra people staying with us, which was a real nightmare for a person who'd just lost his eyesight.

Those early weeks at home left me with a few sad situations I don't think I will ever forget.

Late one night, Kristi awoke to find my side of the bed empty. She put on her robe and began looking for me, whispering my name quietly so she wouldn't disturb the babies. When she peeked into the boys' nursery, she found me lying on the floor between their cribs, crying uncontrollably, as they continued to quietly sleep.

She tried to console me, but I was totally engrossed in mourning all of the things I wouldn't be able to do with my sons. The force of that realization was incomprehensible! I wouldn't be able to play baseball or basketball with them. I wouldn't be able to go skiing with them. I wouldn't be able to go on bike rides or teach them how to play golf. And even worse, I wouldn't be able to *watch them grow up* —or anything else for that matter. The expressions on their faces, school concerts, Boy Scout outings, graduations, weddings, everything would simply be black. I think, for me, that moment may have been the very rock bottom.

Those were some of the most heart wrenching times of my life. I was, of course, totally underestimating my capabilities as a blind dad. In the years since June 1994, I have become more than proficient at accomplishing most of these things with my boys.

૨

One night, a summer monsoon blew into our desert city. I am a native Arizonian and because rain here is so infrequent, I find tranquility in it. I picked up Colton, wrapped him in a blanket, and found my way out to the back patio, where I sat cradling him, waiting for the inevitable wind and rain. Then it came. I will never forget my feelings of desperation and helplessness as the rain and thunder roared around us. As I held him close to my chest, tears rolled down my cheeks and onto his head.

I think Colton somehow knew he was my little anchor that night. In the face of my chaos, fear and hopelessness, he lay in my arms, wide awake, calm and peaceful. In his way, he was telling me that everything was going to work out just fine.

One Saturday morning as I sat resting on the couch, Kristi innocently handed me the newspaper and asked me to hold it. As I felt the paper, which was encircled by a rubber band, I became overwhelmed. On past Saturdays I'd loved reading the newspaper, front to back. Now, it was just a useless weight in my hands. To escape from my painful feelings, I dropped it as if it were fiery hot, got up and groped my way into our bedroom. I often avoided Kristi when I was upset because I didn't want her to see me that way. Sometimes I hid in our bedroom or locked myself in the bathroom. But, in spite of the fact I was trying to hide my feelings from her, it proved fruitless. Kristi could tell when I was heading for a fall, sometimes even before I was aware of it myself.

A couple of weeks after my return home, I got what was one of the most uncomfortable phone calls I have ever received. It was from a good friend, Roberto Guerrieri.

"Hey, how are you doing? I haven't talked with you for a while and I thought I'd call and see what you were up to."

I could tell by his casual demeanor and the context of his question that he was unaware of the accident. Roberto is one of those friends that I only see a couple of times a year. Because I seldom spoke to him and he didn't know any of my other friends I surmised it was possible he had not heard about it.

"You don't know about the accident, do you?" I asked somberly. I then proceeded, as best I could, to tell him about the accident and my subsequent blindness. It was the first time I ever had to tell the story.

At first, Roberto thought I was pulling his leg, a perfectly natural response for him because we had always had a friendly, joking kind of relationship.

I met Roberto while I was living in Tucson, Arizona in the late 1980s. Since I was (and still am) a staunch Arizona State University Sun Devil alumni and supporter, I was living in hostile territory—Tucson is the home of the University of Arizona Wildcats, ASU's arch rival. Roberto and his roommates would heckle me incessantly on the topic. One year, after the Wildcats had beaten the Sun Devils, which squashed the Sun Devils' Rose Bowl hopes for that year, Roberto and the guys taped a huge and smelly bouquet of burnt, plastic roses to my door . . . very funny!

This kind of friendly heckling between Roberto and me had continued over the years. So, as Roberto held the phone to his ear he was waiting for the punch line. Several seconds passed as reality eventually sank in. But once he understood I wasn't joking, Roberto was very sympathetic.

As I hung up, I began to ponder the conversation. It was unnerving to think that this was the first of many times—maybe thousands of times—that I would have to tell someone that I was blind.

The main questions I asked myself during those early days were, "Why me? Why did this have to happen to me? This wasn't supposed to happen! I had plans and dreams and things I wanted to do. Now I had new responsibilities as a father and husband. How was I supposed to do all of this as a blind person?"

Looking back, I can see that my fear, sadness and anger at the hopelessness of my own situation may have overshadowed any resentment I may have felt toward the man who caused the accident-and I have long since forgiven him.

I didn't blame God, the police or anyone else. I was reconciled to the fact that the accident had just 'happened.' I was blind and the rest of my life would be spent in the dark. The sadness felt suffocating!

Simple events of everyday life took on new meaning for me. Listening to traffic reports on the radio, for example, became sad, personal reminders. Whenever an auto accident was reported, I would start thinking about how someone's life has just been ruined.

One Saturday morning, I found myself listening to a cooking program. Why I was tuning into such a program is beyond me, as I have no particular interest in cooking, but there I was. The program's participants were debating the proper wine to be served with steamed clams, and I was thinking, "Who cares?" There are people out there going through life-changing experiences, like me, and these people are bickering about wine selection.

This was, of course, situational depression, but knowing that didn't change anything about my mental state. I was sad and frustrated with the world.

The fact that I was suffering from sleep deprivation didn't help matters, either. The combination of my depression and its attendant insomnia, night feedings for the babies, and my inability to distinguish the difference between day and night (which really screwed up my circadian rhythms for months) created a physical and emotional climate in which I could rarely sleep for more than a couple of hours at a time. It was too much! Well . . . almost.

ॐ

The first stage of recovery from my depression was correcting my sleep patterns. With the help of an antidepressant, shortening my daytime naps, and following the same patterns as the sighted people in my house, I was eventually able to get some much needed sleep. The process took several months and lots of patience on the parts of everyone involved, but it helped to alleviate my depression.

Around this time, Kristi and I also started seeing a psychologist on a regular basis. This proved helpful, too. Our sessions eased my frustration, gave Kristi the extra patience she would need to cope successfully, and helped to keep us on track with our love for each other.

On the other hand, during these visits we discovered Kristi's head injury had been much worse than anyone had initially thought. With all of the attention focused on me and so much being required of Kristi during the crisis period, her mental deficiencies had gone unnoticed. Kristi was finally diagnosed as suffering from memory loss and problems with processing information.

Progress occurred very slowly during the first year. If it were to be traced on a graph, the 'growth chart' would not be consistently upward. First of all, it would have been ragged—two steps forward, one step back—and the angle of upward progress would have seemed almost undetectable, nearly a 'flat line.' At best, things got a little bit better on some days and not too much worse on others. But the longer and more assiduously we worked, *together*, the more pronounced the upward angle!

During this time, I slowly started to get my body back into shape, as well. I was beginning to put on weight—a tall order, since I had lost about 20% of my body weight.

The physical therapist was now coming to our home three times a week. I was still working out with large rubber bands for muscle strengthening and doing various stretching and balancing exercises. As we continued working, the therapist had me get in the swimming pool and do different paddling and resistance routines. I also began riding an exercise bike.

I asked my friend Chris Hahn to take me to the sporting goods store to pick up a bike. Chris was one of my close friends who had kept a vigil on me while I was in the hospital. This would be our first visit in "the real world."

I suspect that being with me was very difficult for Chris at first. I was a friend he'd grown up with, played sports with and been in a rock band with. But, now I was a friend who was dealing with a major disability.

Chris never really talked about his feelings, but I know this guy too well. Besides, someone told me that shortly after the accident, he drove to the site to look around. Because he is so close-mouthed, I can only imagine what must have gone through his mind as he looked at the broken glass and twisted metal that remained, wondering how everything had gone so terribly wrong. He did say that he found a large section of my bumper and couldn't believe it was left there. He thought that the clean-up crew showed disrespect by doing so. But, in spite of how he was dealing with the aftermath, in true Chris Hahn style, this great friend made the 'bike buying' afternoon seem perfectly normal. Thanks Buddy!

A long-time friend, Trent Smock, was another example of a guy who really helped us through the tough times. He was constantly there, trying to help us by running errands, taking us out to lunch, and providing financial and moral support. He was never this nice to me on the basketball court!

On one occasion, Trent sensed we were truly sleep deprived. So, one night, he insisted on staying with us. He told us it was our night off and instructed us to go to our room, get a good night's sleep, and not come out until morning.

It would have been an interesting sight to see. He is a hulk of a guy, he played both football and basketball for Indiana University. He is certainly not what I would consider a nanny type at all—but there he was with two babies and who knows how many bottles and diapers!

While he might not be a 'touchy-feely' guy, he most definitely is a guy with a huge heart.

The truth is, the positive response from almost everyone was overwhelming. We received hundreds of cards and letters from family, friends and people we didn't even know. We were given gifts, items for our boys and financial assistance. A casual business associate, Larry Stuckey, even made monthly deposits into our account.

We were so inundated with calls that many times we had to take the phone off the hook. For 13 weeks after our accident, friends, co-workers and a Sunday school class from Grace Community Church brought us meals almost daily.

Kristi's mom, Connie, really was our "guardian angel" during those early stages after the accident. She stayed with us from the time Kristi was released from the hospital until I returned home and was stabilized. In addition to helping to feed and take care of our premature babies, she took my mom's place in making sure that my nutritional needs were met. All of my meals still needed to be blended, and she diligently performed this chore several times a day. I honestly don't know what we would have done without her love and support during this difficult time.

The incredible outpouring of help and support allowed Kristi and me to conserve our energy for healing. To this day, I am still humbled and grateful for all that was done for us.

Although I received help and support from many outside sources during these difficult days, there is no doubt that God was my ultimate provider and healer. I spent countless hours on my knees, in my bed or lying on the floor, praying to a God I had only recently come to know. At a time when I was more desperate than I had ever thought possible, He was there to lift me up and carry me through the darkness. It was at this time I slowly began to understand that He had bigger plans for me than I had for myself.

Chapter 12

Learning to Accept
My Disability

Slowly but surely, week by week, month by month, I began to feel better about my circumstances. I got to the point where I would only break down a time or two each day. Then I began to string a day or two together with no lapses. Weeks eventually became months, and I was feeling better about my situation.

Along with gaining more control of my emotions, I was successfully accomplishing different tasks around the house. These were relatively small things, but they helped show me that I wasn't helpless. It started with simple things in the kitchen like fixing breakfast and putting away dishes. It was so strange to be performing these tasks without my sight, but the more I did them, the more comfortable and efficient I became.

I then progressed to more complicated jobs. I'm not sure whether I was doing them because they needed to be done or if I just wanted to see if I could do them. These included things like changing the internal parts of a toilet, backwashing the swimming pool, changing the strings on my guitar, and assembling furniture.

On one occasion, I enlisted Kristi to help me mow the yard. I had always done it myself and I saw no reason I couldn't still do it. My plan was to have her stand between my arms and steer while I pushed the mower. This was one hot, summer day after the accident, and she was still wearing a cast on her foot, her clavicles were very weak—and I wasn't exactly healthy, either. What a sight we must have been! We eventually got the lawn mowed, but I decided to have someone else do it from then on.

Aside from the Lord above, Kristi has been the most important part of my healing process. Her influence was never more apparent than it was in those early months after my release from the hospital.

First, she wanted to help me re-establish that I was the head of the house. This is a Christian principle that is important to us. We did need to develop some new ground rules about who was to do what in our little organization. Our circumstances now dictated that she take over some of the responsibilities that were previously mine, such as driving the car and paying the bills. Those weren't hard to take because they made good common sense. But we knew that we had to be wary of her becoming my caregiver.

When we discussed these issues, I found that her trust in me helped build my self-esteem. I would hold up my end in whatever ways I could, and she knew it. It also showed that she trusted me with another critical Christian belief that goes hand in hand: to love and honor your wife.

As this element of our relationship developed, I again began to see myself as an important part of the family unit, not just a disabled member who needed to be taken care of. I had to once again become the head of our home.

The other crucial thing Kristi did (or I should say, didn't do) was try to help me too much. The natural response for most people when they interact with a disabled person is to attempt to do everything for them; they want to perform the simplest task so the disabled person doesn't have to.

This is, of course, the exact opposite of what the disabled person needs. Whenever possible, the disabled person should be accomplishing the task by himself, even if it takes longer. Doing everything for a disabled person renders him more helpless, causing feelings of incompetence and worthlessness.

Kristi spent many hours 'sitting on her hands', as she says, watching as I awkwardly tried to complete some simple task. For the most part, she would not assist me until I asked for it. This, she observes, was excruciatingly difficult at times. I broke so many glasses, I started using plastic cups. I ran into coffee tables on a regular basis and had the bruised shins to prove it.

As a result of her hands-off approach, I slowly began to build self-confidence by accomplishing tasks on my own. If Kristi had not stepped back and allowed me to take care of myself when I could, there is no doubt in my mind that I would have become a more dependant person.

Today, to Kristi's delight, I am very adept at many household duties. I do dishes, cook meals, take out garbage, wash, dry and fold laundry, vacuum carpets and clean off countertops, all on a regular basis. I also make freshly ground coffee every morning and bring Kristi a hot cup while she is getting ready for her day. Many of our female friends tell me they wish I would teach their husbands how to do some of these chores (for obvious reasons). I get a certain amount of satisfaction from being told that I am more helpful around the house than husbands who can see.

There are, however, some household jobs which experience has taught me I'm better off leaving to Kristi. Some examples? Sorting clothes, matching socks, and paying bills.

Getting proficient with chores around the house may sound like a small thing, but it was huge to me. It gave me a sense of worth in our home and made me feel like I carried my share of the load. Who would have thought that doing the dishes could be so rewarding?

Outside the house, I also began taking on some activities that helped with my emotional healing. The way I did things had to change, but at least I could still do them.

We bought a tandem bike, which proved entertaining. At first, it was very strange to be riding along without being able to see or steer, but I soon got accustomed to it. Today I am more comfortable with it than Kristi is. And for several years, I rode with friends in a Tucson to Phoenix charity event. At the end of each event, I asked myself the same question: "Why did I do this?" One hundred miles *is a long way!* By the next year, though, I had forgotten the aches and pains, and would do it again.

One year, when I was riding with my friend Armando Miranda, we missed the scheduled lunch stop. We decided to detour off to a family Mexican restaurant in a small town called Eloy, about 25 miles from the end of the ride. One Corona led to another, and it was two hours before we got out of there. On the way out, I stepped off a curb and twisted my ankle, making the remainder of the ride a bit more interesting than we had planned. But—and this is important—we finished the race.

A sad side note: In October of 2003, Armando died suddenly of acute leukemia, leaving behind his wife Caroline and their two children, Alyssa and Austin. It was another reminder to appreciate each day that we are given.

Chapter 13

Leeza Gibbons Visits Our Home

Two days after the accident, our episode of the Leeza Gibbons show aired. Someone had already called Leeza to tell her what had happened to us. She tried to contact us while we were in the hospital, but she never got through. So she and her staff monitored our progress by talking to other family members. She sent us notes and gifts, which really helped to lift our spirits. My summation of Leeza had been correct. She was a person of good integrity, genuinely concerned for us and our well-being.

A couple of weeks after my discharge from the hospital, Leeza called to check on us. I was both surprised and pleased when I heard her voice on the phone. I have always been impressed that she called personally, instead of delegating the job to an assistant.

We had an easy, casual conversation. She was just calling to see how we were handling it.

Several weeks later, she called again, asking us if we would be interested in doing a follow-up show. After Kristi and I discussed it, we told her we would.

From the time we did the first show, we felt like we were part of Leeza's TV family. She and her staff always treated us with respect and we never felt exploited.

Because of our fragile medical conditions, there was no way we could travel to Los Angeles. So Leeza came to our house! She showed up with her camera and sound crew early one morning. It was an emotional reunion. We talked honestly and openly about our trauma, (including the worst of our worries and disappointments), as she sat on our family room floor. She really put us at ease, so much so, that we spent half of the day just talking with her and showing off our new babies.

She put together an entire, hour-long show devoted to our tribulations . . . and triumphs. When it aired, about a month after it was recorded, Kristi and I were not ready for what we saw. We didn't know the show would include footage of our accident scene. As we watched, I heard Kristi gasp and then start crying as they showed the twisted, mangled Jeep. Kristi was so emotional that she simply couldn't put words to what she was seeing. A friend had to explain it to me.

In the years between then and now, we have appeared on Leeza's show many times. For a couple of episodes, we went to Los Angeles with the boys to film in the studio. On one show, Leeza had a film crew follow me around for a day. They filmed me at work, golfing, swimming with the boys, and riding a tandem bike with Kristi. I must admit, I felt a bit like a trained monkey.

One year, shortly after I returned from a snow skiing trip, we went to Los Angeles to film an episode. Jill Milliken-Bates, Leeza's producer, joked with me that I might not be too happy with their selection of the skiing footage.

As it turns out, they had included some moments when I was crashing. I felt embarrassed; I thought that America must now think that the blind guy was a lousy skier. We had provided the footage from our home video camera. Silly me! Next time I'll edit the material before I send it out.

I think our story appealed to Leeza and her viewers over the years because they witnessed us overcoming our tragedy. And I think that Leeza's involvement in our lives helped us in our healing process by giving us a more objective view Personally, this produced hope, excitement about the possibilities, and even a strengthening of my faith, both in myself and in others.

Whenever we did a show, it served as a reminder to me that even though we had been through a traumatic ordeal, we had survived—no, thrived. Many times, this helped me to put our challenges into perspective. It has also helped me to see how well we've really done.

Leeza, at one point, offered us a contract with her production company to be a part of a motion picture about our "adventures." Unfortunately, the project was never picked up by a network, but I learned that this is not unusual—less than one project in several hundred is ever picked up by a commercial production house or television network. Nevertheless, I joked to Kristi that it was my fault; if I'd done something stupid and cruel, like thrown goldfish into the Jacuzzi, the Lifetime network would have signed us in a heartbeat.

Even though Leeza's show is no longer on the air, we still maintain contact with her. She has gone on to work with Alzheimer's patients and their caregivers, a generous and worthy cause she personally understands all too well. I cannot put into words how valuable her friendship and support has been.

Chapter 14

Loss of Other Senses

One day, while Kristi was shopping, she bought some Jelly Belly candies. These tasty little candies are quite unique, with bizarre but tasty flavors which include watermelon, jalapeño, bubble gum and lemon, just to name a few. Amazed at the flavor explosion that each candy delivered, Kristi began handing me one jellybean at a time to see if I could distinguish the difference. To my disappointment, I couldn't.

Our next visit to my neurologist confirmed what I had already suspected. I had lost my sense of smell and taste in the accident. The trauma from the impact had damaged the olfactory nerves. These nerves provide the sense of smell, which in turn is a major factor in providing the sense of taste.

With all of the other deprivations going on in my life, I had chosen to ignore this one. My sense of taste and smell was never acute, due to allergies, so I convinced myself that these senses would eventually return to their 'normal', below-average state.

Interestingly (probably because it had never been really important to me), the idea that chicken and fish would forever taste the same left me somewhat unaffected. As a family, our lives did not revolve around meals, so I was sure I could live with this inconvenience of "sub-standard" taste buds.

I was much more negatively affected by the loss of smell. The thought of never being able to enjoy the crisp, clean smell of rain or the robust aroma of freshly ground coffee was depressing. Worse, smell was a sense I could have relied more on because of my blindness. It could have helped me orient myself in a room or an outdoor environment, as well as provide me with a reference point based on that sensory pleasure of my memory. Sure, there are a lot of foul odors out there, and I certainly hadn't missed those, but I would have taken the trade-off in a minute. There was no way to correct this loss, or so I thought. I simply had to accept it.

A few years after the accident, I started seeing an acupuncturist because I had read articles about treatments to help the optic nerve, and I thought I'd give it a try. I had never really been a believer in acupuncture and similar, non-allopathic treatments, but truth be told, I never bothered to learn much about them. The sessions did nothing to improve my vision—but what is that smell?

A couple of months into my treatments, just as I was becoming discouraged with my acupuncture regimen and its lack of results, I went on a camping trip with my dad and brother. We were cooped up in a tiny travel trailer, in the middle of nowhere, in the southern Arizona desert. It was very confining and offered almost no ventilation, and my Dad was cooking in the kitchen. Then I smelled it! He was cooking chili!! That chili was the best chili I'd ever tasted!

As it turns out, I did get back some sense of smell and taste, not quite as acute as it was before the accident, but I guarantee you, it's much better than nothing. I don't know whether the acupuncture actually made the difference, but I give it the credit.

People often ask me if my other senses have improved since I lost my sight. My standard answer is that they are not any better; I just pay more attention to them. Since I am not bombarded with the visual input of a sighted person, I can concentrate on the remaining senses, primarily hearing.

After years of trying to convince my wife (and myself) that my hearing was just fine, thank you very much, I reluctantly agreed to have it tested. When the results confirmed what Kristi already knew, I had to admit that my failed rock and roll career and an unfortunate firecracker accident had permanently damaged my hearing. Luckily, the majority of the loss was in only one ear and a hearing aid quickly solved the problem. I hadn't realized what I was missing until I had it back.

In 2001, I fell prey to a nifty little malady called Bell's palsy. This condition left half my face paralyzed. My doctor explained to me that the virus that causes this malady may lie dormant in the system for years, flaring up during times of extreme stress, when the immune system is suppressed.

Quite frankly, Bell's Palsy has created many problems for me. Of those afflicted with it, only 70% achieve full recovery. Of the remaining 30%, about half achieve no recovery at all. And half, like me, get back only limited facial movement. This has proven to be quite a challenge.

My primary concern when first stricken was my speech. In the initial phases, my speech was slurred and my lip drooped noticeably. I was worried that I wouldn't be able to continue my public speaking. Fortunately, the minimal movement I have gotten back has been around my mouth. Now, my speech is impeded only when I am tired. I still have to deal with other issues, though. Simple tasks like drinking from a glass with a straw, eating, brushing my teeth and shaving all require special attention. One positive thing to come out of it, as far as Kristi is concerned, is that I can no longer whistle. She hated it when I whistled.

Another result of Bell's Palsy is that I can no longer close my right eye, so I sometimes wear a patch. Kristi says that my patches make me look rather dapper. So I now own suede patches in several different colors, from which I can choose to match my attire. I also have some 'fun' patches for holidays like Christmas and Halloween, and some 'specialty' patches I can wear to baseball games and when I play golf. I even have one patch with an American flag on it, for patriotic events, and another with dice on it, to be worn on trips to Las Vegas and when I make insurance sales presentations to major companies (just kidding on that last one)!

People who don't know me are sometimes confused by this fashion statement. They often assume since I have a patch over one eye, the other eye must work fine. At times, I am tempted to wear patches over both eyes to alleviate the confusion, but I'm afraid that would destroy the fashion statement.

As an alternative, I wear sunglasses. This seems to do one of two things; it alerts observant people that I am blind (a la Stevie Wonder) or that I am a famous celebrity (a la Stevie Wonder). Either way, not a bad place to be.

Chapter 15

Fatherhood

I n my early days as a father, I made a decision that still affects my role today. I never wanted my boys to feel they had been deprived of anything because their father was blind. Moreover, I never wanted them to feel sorry for me or be embarrassed. I wanted them to think they had the best dad in the world who just happened to be blind.

Generally speaking, I am a pretty involved father. For the first year, I was not working, so I was home full time with the boys. In that respect, the accident provided a beneficial side effect—not many Dads get to be home with their babies full-time.

I learned how to prepare formula, and I fed them on a regular basis, including night feedings. This wasn't really such a difficult duty for me; I was usually up several hours during the night, anyway.

Sometimes I would accidentally hold the bottle nipple side up. Colton would quickly figure out the problem and help me turn it around. Dylan, on the other hand, would just get frustrated and start crying because he couldn't find the nipple. That would be my clue something was wrong.

One day, several months after I got home from the hospital, we hit a milestone when Kristi left me at home, in charge of the boys, 'solo' for the first time, while she went to the grocery store. I know she must have been a nervous wreck, but she tried to appear as calm as possible. I was nervous, too, but I wanted to prove—both to Kristi and myself—that taking care of my sons was something I could do.

I put them in the middle of the family room on a blanket. After starting a Disney video, I sat between them. I then placed a hand on their backs so I could keep track of them. They had not yet hit the crawling stage, and that made my job a lot easier.

I'm sure she was gone for only a short period of time, but to me it seemed like an eternity. Fortunately, I was able to "watch" the boys with no major disasters. They were both still alive and no worse for the wear when she returned. I breathed a silent sigh of relief. I think we both did.

Eventually, I felt confident enough to watch the boys for long periods of time with no more stress than any other father would have faced watching toddler twins. Bathing them, putting them down for naps and, yes, even changing diapers became a part of my repertoire. (I will leave it to your imagination how a blind person changes diapers.)

Once I became comfortable supervising our sons, I started to really enjoy what I saw as our "special time" together. It was just the Welker boys and their Dad playing around the house. Of course, at that age they had no clue that I was blind, nor could they know what that meant. They just wanted to play, eat, sleep and be loved—all things I could easily do.

I think that Colton was the first to figure out I was blind. I noticed he would put a toy (directly) in my hand. He would also grab my hand and pull me over to a place in the room where he wanted me to be. In other words, he seemed to know that he had to be the guide in certain situations. I'm not sure he related all this to my lack of sight, but I do know that at some point he started taking advantage of that fact. One morning I put a handful of Cheerios on his tray. He slid the ones he didn't want to the sides of the tray and said, "Done, Daddy." He took my hand and ran it over the clean portion of the tray directly in front of him. This only worked one time, though. As soon as I removed the tray and carried it to the sink for washing, I discovered his two little piles of Cheerios, one on each edge.

Much later—when he was about three or four—he tried to pull a similar stunt. I had given both Colton and Dylan a slice of pizza, then I left the room. I was gone for less than a minute, and when I returned, Dylan was still eating but Colton was playing. When I questioned Colton, he told me he had finished his pizza. Of course, that didn't compute. Knowing that a whole slice of pizza couldn't disappear into a little boy in that short a time, I checked the garbage can and found a slice of pizza with one bite missing. I was both disappointed and tickled. I'm sure he was completely dumbfounded when I confronted him. I wish I could have seen the look on his face when he realized I knew where the uneaten pizza was stashed.

I really enjoyed the bedtime ritual we started early on. After they brushed their teeth and said their prayers, it was story time. The boys would have me go through an exhaustive list of stories so they could pick one out. These were stories I made up, mostly. Some were really goofy, but the boys loved to hear them.

After the story, it was lights out and time for bed. I would always lie down with Dylan first and he would quickly fall sound asleep. Colton, on the other hand, was another story. He was fidgety, wouldn't stop talking and would come up with a thousand reasons not to go to sleep. (Experts would probably tell parents it's best to let their children fall asleep on their own. What do they know?)

Eventually, Colton would run out of gas and I would hear only the rhythmic breathing of these two little gifts from God. As I lay with my serene angels, I knew all was right with the world. The Lord had entrusted us with these gifts, and that gave me purpose.

Over the years, the boys have said many times they thought I could see and was just faking it. When they were still very young I would usually give them a vague response to their queries just to keep them guessing. I needed every advantage I could get-still do.

In the spirit of full disclosure, I must admit that Kristi and I did have some help from nannies in the early years of the boy's lives. In all honesty, I don't know how we would have gotten by without the help of these ladies. With the ongoing fallout from our head injuries, adapting to my blindness, and Kristi adjusting to her new role as a caregiver, the nannies made the parenting process much easier.

Eva Villa, an au pair from Mexico, here on a cultural exchange program, was a very special nanny to us. Eva became a beloved member of our family, and we still keep in touch with her on a regular basis. She holds a place in our hearts, but initially the relationship was tenuous at best.

The first time we left the boys alone with Eva, we returned to find a stand-off going on in the living room. Eva was sitting on one couch crying, and our defiant three year olds sons were sitting, arms crossed, on the opposing couch. As soon as we entered the room, they blurted out, "We want Eva to go back to Mexico. Now!"

We quickly defused the confrontation and, thankfully, the scene was not indicative of "coming attractions." Eva turned out to be a warm, loving person and we are truly blessed to have her in our life.

One of the boy's sitters, Khara Fuentes, is also very much a part of our family. Khara was only 15 years-old when she started babysitting the boys. Kristi refers to her as our "surrogate daughter." We've watched her grow and mature into a young woman, now working toward her Masters in Counseling.

&

Today, the boys are very good at filling me in on visual details so I can paint a picture in my mind. They describe their artwork to me and provide play-by- play descriptions of the games we watch.

Dylan never misses an opportunity to explain the facial expressions of a dog or what his hamster is up to. He also has me put my hands on his body so I can feel his style for hitting and pitching a baseball.

Colton is great at taking my hand to demonstrate what he is doing on his skateboard or bike. He will often have me stand up so he can put my body into awkward positions to tell me all about his most recent wipe-out.

Both boys draw designs on my hand, arm or chest to describe something to me. For more complex diagrams, like logos, they use 'the chest method' as their drawing board. They have also become excellent sighted guides, although Colton does tend to get distracted at times and walk me into things.

Consistent with my focus on what can be done rather than what can't, I'm always willing to try out a new activity or "visualization." It's quite amazing how many activities I can do with the boys. I often surprise other people—and sometimes I surprise myself!

Since they were very young, I have wrestled with my sons. I taught them the Roman Greco start position, some of the basic moves, and the three-second pin. These matches are anything but regulation, of course, but we have a blast. I usually start in the down position with one son on each side. The contest then pretty much turns into a tag team melee, with me ending up on the bottom of the pile. I know that one day they'll get too big for all this, but I'll take it for as long as I can.

Swimming is a big part of our summer activities in Arizona. Since they learned to swim, I've enjoyed playing with the boys in our pool. 'Marco Polo' was obviously a popular game, but I always had to be 'it'. We also played pirates on a raft and went under the waterfall. For another popular game, I would swim underwater, with one of the boys holding on around my neck for as long as he could. We also horsed around, and I would throw them into the deep end or have them get on my shoulders and play sea monster. After they tired me out, I would sit at the edge of the pool and listen to them very intently. I could have no distractions such as telephone calls, or background sounds such as music, as I had to focus my undivided attention on them. Every few seconds, I would ask them something to get a verbal response so I could keep track and confirm their locations.

These days, they can both swim circles around me. Now I just sit in the shade in a lounge chair, drink my soda pop, try to stay dry, and listen for major rule infractions—tricks like putting all of our dogs on a raft, jumping off of the rock waterfall, or taking baseball bats into the pool. I discovered all of these activities—and more—by listening very closely.

There was one right of passage that was a real challenge—teaching our sons how to ride a bike. This can be a terrifying time in any parent's life. And the terror is mathematically doubled if you have twins, quadrupled if one of the parents is blind.

I was really worried, Kristi was nervous, Dylan was terrified, and Colton pretty much thought he could do it by himself. That is how it was when Kristi and I taught the boys to ride bikes.

Oh, sure, at first they had training wheels. But those things can do more harm than good. The problem is; they allow the rider to fall for a split second before the training wheel touches the ground and gives them stability. Kids soon figure out that they will have a more secure ride if they tilt the bike to one side from the get-go. This is a bad technique, and it doesn't work at all when the training wheels are removed. Between Kristi and me, though, we succeeded. Somehow, and I honestly don't remember how, they learned to ride. Now they ride all over the place, go off jumps, do wheelies and bunny hops (whatever those are) and don't give it a second thought. As they say, 'it's just like riding a bike.'

Being typical boys, anything with wheels on it is now fair game. Taking up space in our garage are: skateboards, roller blades, scooters, and several other multi-wheeled devices I can't identify.

The other day, I actually got on Dylan's skateboard and discovered that I could still do a 360. Agog, Dylan said, "Wow, Dad! I can't even do that!"

Yes!

Basketball was my favorite sport to play when I could see. This is another activity we have been able to modify so I can play with my sons. I attach a small radio to the bottom of the basket's rim, which has been lowered. This allows me to "hear" where the rim is.

One day, Colton and I were playing 'horse' and he was making everything he put up, or so I thought. I was starting to get suspicious, and when he told me he made one that didn't make any noise at all, I questioned him on it. He eventually confessed that several of his shots had not, in fact, gone in. As I recall, that little deception got him grounded for a week.

Both boys, especially Dylan, love baseball. Traditional hitting and catching is out for me, so we have come up with some alternatives. I will have one son play the field while I throw fly balls and grounders to him. He will then throw the ball back to his brother, who stands next to me.

For hitting practice, I took a bag of tennis balls to the mound and pitched to one son while the other played the field. I would have the batter talk so I would know where to throw. We had only limited success with this method and eventually discontinued it. The first problem was; it was hard to find the strike zone. Then the boys started to hit the ball harder—and there I stood, a 'sitting *blind* duck.' Ouch!

The boys have gone on to play little league, and they really enjoy it. Although I am disappointed that I can't be their coach, as I had planned, I do appreciate the Dads who donate their time and effort to do it. Kristi and I rarely miss a game, but I am always a bit torn with emotions. On the one hand, I am proud to see them develop in the game I loved as a kid. On the other hand, their developing skills serve as a painful reminder of what I cannot see.

A few years ago, we bought an air-hockey table. During a series of visits to a local, air-hockey-equipped pizza parlor I had figured out a way to play the game (sort of). I'm sure what I do is cheating, but who cares? Once the puck comes to my side of the rink, I grab it with my free hand and set up my shot with the paddle. I have gotten pretty good at shooting from this vantage point. Every once in a while I can score a nice, clean goal.

As is frequently the case with these purchases, the boys played quite a bit at first, but then the table began to gather dust. It then served as a spacious, albeit expensive, table for an elaborate hamster cage for Napoleon and Terminator. After the hamsters' funerals, it got used only by Colton and Dylan's friends.

Most traditional board and video games are not accessible to me, so we have invented verbal games to take their place. These include some very elaborate games such as "Guess the MLB Baseball Player" and "The Guessing Game," with categories such as animals, movies, cars and cartoon characters.

We played the "Guess the MLB Baseball Player" game so much that Kristi wouldn't play it with us anymore. She really wasn't very good at it anyway. This was probably because she only knew four players.

We have a Monopoly game that was specially designed for the blind. All of the properties are marked with raised lines, the money and cards are noted in Braille, and the dice have protruding dots. These modifications allow me to play Monopoly with no assistance (a game I really loved when I was young).

We also have other specially adapted games such as tic-tac-toe, checkers, chess, and even a tennis racquet that allows the contestant to play a computer-generated match using sound effects.

Kristi and I have been diligent about taking pictures and videos at every opportunity. I often pull out the camcorder to do the filming myself. I figure it's better to have some less-than-perfect footage than none at all. Who knows, if I ever get my sight back (or if they ever discover a way to beam images into my brain), I can re-live these special moments.

Contrary to what I thought, I have learned that it's not so much the *quality* of the time you spend with your children, but the *quantity*. Sure, I'm not great at baseball or basketball, but the time I spend with my sons is absolutely irreplaceable.

Chapter 16

Getting Out and Keeping Active

While not a sports fanatic, I have always enjoyed watching my favorite teams play. Before the accident, I went to the Phoenix Suns, Arizona Cardinals, and Arizona State University games. It disheartened me to think about attending those activities without my sight. "What's the purpose?" I thought.

A year after the accident, I attended my first sporting event. Kristi, the boys, my in-laws and I went to a rodeo. I had never been to a rodeo, but my father-in-law was a cattle rancher and we thought the boys would enjoy it.

I wasn't at all sure what I would glean from this experience. It seemed that to just sit there and see nothing would be as boring as watching grass grow. On the other hand, I didn't want to stay home by myself.

Several weeks before the rodeo, I had promised myself not to fall into the trap that so many blind people fall victim to. I simply would not become a shut-in. Regardless of the cost; I wasn't going to become a prisoner in my own home.

For the rodeo, I brought along a radio with headphones. I figured that while everyone was watching the action, I could listen to talk radio. After about 15 minutes of doing this, I realized it was not the answer. I felt isolated, almost as though I wasn't really there with the group. I felt detached, not involved in the activity.

At that point, I removed the headphones and sat there in the dark, listening to the rodeo. Although I still felt depressed about not being able to see what was going on, at least I felt involved with my family.

Although I am not a rodeo fan and knew virtually nothing about the events, at least I was there.

About an hour into the rodeo, a lady sitting in front of us turned around. "I hope I'm not bothering you," she asked," but weren't you two just on the Leeza Gibbons show?"

She had seen the follow-up Leeza show. She went on to tell us how inspirational our story was and how excited she was to meet us.

It was rewarding to hear how our story affected others. It was also uplifting for a stranger to offer words of encouragement. Situations similar to this continue to this day, and they always make me feel like I am doing something right, something worthwhile.

The first team-sport event I attended after the accident was a Phoenix Suns game. Dr. Travis Holcombe and his wife Kathy asked Kristi and me to go. Since the Suns games are broadcast on the radio, I brought a portable with me. Surprisingly, I was actually looking forward to the game. With the help of the radio, I would be able to follow the play-by-play action. Travis, however, had other plans.

As the game began, I pulled out my headphones and started to put them on. "What are you going to do with those?" Travis asked.

I told him I planned on listening to the game.

"Would it be OK if I called the action for you? I've always wanted to be a sports announcer," Travis asked.

I put away my radio and listened as he described the game. As it turned out, he wasn't too bad. I told him if his medical career didn't work out, he might have a future in the broadcasting booth.

During the game, he relayed to me that Mohammad Ali was in attendance. He was sitting courtside with a friend of Travis'. At halftime, he asked me if I wanted to meet him. Before I knew it, I was shaking hands with the Champ. I was thrilled.

By this point in Ali's life, he was well into the later stages of Parkinson's disease. He was in Phoenix for a fundraising event. A wing of the Barrows Neurological Center, the same center in which I had my surgeries, was being dedicated to him.

As if meeting the greatest boxer of all time wasn't enough, Travis asked if I'd like to stop by the Suns locker room. "Yeah, sure," I answered casually, as if that's what I usually did at halftime.

As we circulated through the locker room, Travis introduced me to some of the staff and coaches. Among others, we chatted with the late Cotton Fitzsimmons, the former head coach of the Suns. I had met him a couple of times before and had always walked away with the same impression; he was as amiable a guy face-to-face as he was in the spotlight.

As we sat there during the second half, I remember thinking, "Sure, I can't see the game with my eyes, but I'm enjoying the event with different senses." I was also meeting some great people I otherwise would never have met.

Today, Kristi and I have season tickets for ASU Sun Devil football. To be honest, my favorite part is the tailgate parties before each game. Football is a pretty good radio sport, and my enjoyment level usually tracks with how well the team is playing. I have been going to ASU games since the early 1970's. You see, I can support my Alma matter, blind or not.

We also share a season ticket package for the Phoenix Suns. I really like the team, but basketball is not a very good radio sport. I know too much about the game and its hidden intricacies. When I could see, I often would watch the action away from the ball. But because the game moves so fast, the announcer can only call the critical plays, so I miss the details that made it so interesting.

There are two other major problems with attending basketball games. First, the radio reception is often poor because it is broadcast via closed circuit. Second, the crowd gets so vociferous at critical junctures, I can't hear the play. Even with those drawbacks, though, I still enjoy going to Suns games.

My absolute favorite sporting event is an Arizona Diamondbacks game at Chase Field. Due to the slow-paced nature of the game and the echo-filled, expansive stadium, baseball is by far the best radio sport. To be there in person adds an exciting dimension. The strategies and gamesmanship involved in baseball keep it interesting and entertaining.

And the announcers, who are real aficionados, pay attention to the tactics and report them fully, which gives me everything I need for a great game experience.

You should see me at the ballpark! Since I'm listening to the radio, I often provide critical information for those fans sitting around me. I'm an unending source of baseball statistics!

While I was growing up, I played a lot of baseball and followed the major leagues closely. By the time I reached college, though, other activities captured my attention and I lost most of my interest. Then, a few years after the accident, the Diamondbacks organization was established, and I was hooked from the first spring training.

Chase Field provides excellent accessible seating for the disabled. I even have my own, private usher, Leroy. It makes the experience much more enjoyable. On the weekends, Kristi, the boys and I often attend Saturday night games. My mom, dad and brother Jim and I go to the weekday afternoon 'businessman's special' games.

During the boys' spring break, we often go to spring training baseball games. The Cactus League plays in the Phoenix metro area, and we get to watch some of the best teams and players in the world. I'm sure Kristi would rather be lounging on a beach in California, but she never complains. Is she a great mom/wife, or what?

Attending sporting events is now a normal part of our social life, and I have learned to appreciate it regardless of the fact that I can't see. I enjoy going to the games for the ambiance: to feel the energy of the crowd, breathe the crisp air, smell the aroma of the grass—and eat food that only tastes good at the ballpark.

I don't want to get too "mushy" about baseball, but these times with my wife, my boys, my parents and my brother are very special to me. We boys go because we love baseball. The girls go because they love their boys. How in the world did I get so lucky?

ଛ

One of the major problems that many blind people have is keeping active. Because they cannot handle tasks that may require unrestricted movement or physical flexibility, many become sedentary. It's all too common to find blind people who have become housebound. They waste away their days sitting on the couch, listening to the radio.

After the accident, I soon realized why the sedentary life is so tempting. The comfort and safety of my home provided security. It was obvious what a dangerous trap it could become. Why go out in public and embarrass myself when I could just sit in the comfort of my living room and avoid it? What a great argument for doing absolutely nothing!

At first, Kristi and I tried to work out at health clubs, but it wasn't effective. It was always a hassle to get there. Once there, it was a challenge to get a trainer to help me. Kristi tried to walk me through my workout, but it was awkward.

The exercise bike was my first step to physical activity. Prior to the accident, I had no use for this boring machine. I belonged to a health club where I did weight training. I got my cardiovascular exercise from basketball. Today, the exercise bike is my main form of cardiovascular work, and I've even grown to like it (well . . . tolerate it, at least). The bike is easy to use and requires nothing other than the motivation to do it. I also have a small weight training room in my home.

In my workout room, I know exactly where the equipment is and how to use it. The convenience of not needing to find transportation to the club is also an attractive part of the arrangement. Personal trainers help me with my program and keep me motivated. Having all of this at my disposal does not mean that I am a muscle-bound guy with an incredible cardiovascular system. Motivation is no easier for me than for most people. What it does mean, however, is that I manage to keep myself in decent shape. I've been able to avoid the weight gain and poor conditioning that plagues so many blind people.

While I have had to give up many of the sports I played, like basketball and tennis, I have found others I can play with a little help, like golf.

Being in the insurance profession, I played golf quite often. Notice that I said I played often, not that I was very good at it. I had a great swing and looked like a golfer, but that is where the talent ended. I didn't have the time (or patience) to learn to play well; I figured I would get serious about it when I retired.

After I lost my sight, I began to hear about blind golfers. At first, the idea seemed a bit improbable. The concept of accurately striking a golf ball without the benefit of sight seemed all but impossible. I had trouble enough trying to get the ball where I wanted it to go when I could see the darned thing.

Initially, friends designed different contraptions to help me. One customized a large plastic mat with built-in ridges and depressions that set up my stance and placed the ball in a set position. Another devised a complicated rig which involved the use of a laser beam sensor that was supposed to help me gauge where the club head was. Although these ideas were well intentioned, they really didn't work, making the whole affair more exasperating.

My friend Doug Carr sensed my frustration. He suggested that we go to the driving range and try hitting some balls without assistance from special gadgets. After I finally got accustomed to not seeing the ball (although I found myself 'visualizing' it), I began to hit it with regularity and often with considerable force. It wasn't long before I thought to myself, "I may be able to do this."

Logically, it makes sense. The golf swing is a repetitive movement that changes very little from club to club. If I could improve my swing, I could have some success. So I continued to practice and to learn, and over time I've gotten better and better. I still need help with many aspects of play, such as direction and distance, but that is to be expected. I am further encouraged since I discovered that there are a number of accomplished golfers who just happen to be blind.

Along with practice came new golf clubs. The new technology incorporated in clubs with larger titanium heads, graphite shafts and improved design has helped to simplify the game for the average golfer, and I've found that it has made the sport easier and more fun for me, too. My golf game is now better than ever. My friends tell me that all of my drives go 250 yards straight down the middle, and I haven't hit into a sand trap in 10 years. (Well, that's what they tell me!)

But seriously, I really have learned to appreciate the game for what it is: an opportunity to spend an afternoon with my friends. I'm still not a 'pro' and I need to take some more lessons, but every once in a while I hit a great shot.

My blindness has led to some interesting situations on the golf course. During one such outing, on the seventh fairway of a course in Puerto Vallarta, Mexico, I encountered a bit more excitement than I'd planned.

My brother-in-law, Joe Sauer, stopped the cart so he could hit his second shot. After walking about 20 feet toward his ball, he returned to the cart and suggested that I stay there until he got back.

"There is an alligator about 30 feet from the cart," he calmly told me. "It doesn't look like it's going anywhere, but I thought I should tell you."

Listening carefully for alligator sounds, I nervously waited until he returned.

Chapter 17

Dreams

My vivid dreams, which started shortly after the accident and continue to this day, have been an interesting phenomenon.

Before I lost my sight, I was, at best, an occasional—and boring—dreamer. My dreams, for the most part, were rather slow moving, uninteresting, and lacked action. I don't even remember whether I dreamed in color or black and white; I only know I dreamed 'dull'. I would dream about going to work all night long, or driving a car on a long trip.

After I'd been home from the hospital for just a few nights, though, I started having very different, very strange dreams. They were visions of huge sheets of color. They'd start in that twilight zone right after I fell asleep. It would be only one color a night and would cover the entire scope of my vision. The colors were so vivid, they looked like wet paint. The odd thing was that these "dreams" lasted for only a couple of weeks and then never happened again. That was fine with me, however, because it was so disturbing. At the time, I thought it was my visual cortex's way of showing my brain these colors for the last time.

Later, I started dreaming about various activities I had engaged in when I could see. In those dreams, I had my vision, but sometimes I would be carrying a white cane. The dreams were very odd; people would refer to me as blind, but I could see.

Today, I dream for hours on end about stocking groceries. These are throwbacks to my old dreams, I think. Stocking grocery store shelves was the job that put me through college. It is repetitive work and there is a seemingly unending supply of merchandise that must get stocked before the store opens. By the time I wake up, I am exhausted; stocking shelves is hard work! These dreams are rewarding, though, because I can see a job well done.

In one of my most common dreams, I am snow skiing for what seems to be the entire night. I can clearly see the robust, green trees against the fresh, white snow and powder blue sky. The runs are impossibly steep and the lift chairs are a thousand feet in the air. Kristi has said maybe that I feel as if I am standing on the edge of the steep cliff of life, fearing an imminent fall. I can't really disagree with her. It's a bit like the feeling you get when you are leaning back in a chair that is just about ready to fall backward.

In another frequent dream, I am driving a ski boat I once owned with my friend Chris Hahn. This was no ordinary ski boat. It was a flat-bottomed, jet-drive machine with a 455-cubic-inch engine. In the dream, I'm flying along the lake at 70 miles per hour with not a care in the world. Kristi probably thinks this means that I am anxious to get to my destination in life. I think it just means I like to go fast.

Often I am golfing in my dreams. I can see, but everyone, including me, thinks I am blind. It's all rather confusing. Everything is vivid: the green fairway, the blue water and white golf balls. I am guided around the course, and my shots are set-up by my friends, but I see everything that's going on. I usually hit the ball pretty well and everyone comments that I'm "a pretty good golfer, for a blind guy." I think to myself, "This isn't so hard." Unfortunately, in my dreams, as in real life, I am still slicing the ball a bit.

Sometimes, in my golf dreams, I am playing impossibly difficult courses, like holes set on the side of huge cliffs in the Grand Canyon. In these dreams, I have to address the ball in precarious positions to get set up for a shot. Like the snow skiing dreams, I am sure this is related to the fact that I sometimes feel as though I am living on the edge.

Curiously, I don't often dream of Colton and Dylan. When I do, I'm in normal settings and I don't find it unusual to see them. The boys always look the same, but their faces are no less detailed than anyone's faces are in my dreams. I think this is God's way of allowing me to see my boys. I'm sure if I ever got my sight back, I could pick them out of a crowd. Kristi is not often in my dreams, either. Whenever she does make an appearance, though, she is at least as pretty as the last time I saw her—maybe even prettier!

Chapter 18

Meeting Stevie Wonder

Bill Smith, a long-time friend, was a regular visitor when I was camped out at St. Joseph's Hospital. I think he came to see me almost every day. Bill is in the restaurant business, so his mornings are flexible. On these a.m. visits he would occasionally sit with me while I was muscling my way through my physical therapy sessions.

One morning, Bill told me that a manager for Stevie Wonder was a friend of his, and he promised to get Stevie and me together sometime. I figured he was just trying to cheer me up, and I promptly forgot the conversation. Oddly, though, over the next few weeks I received a couple of messages saying that Stevie Wonder was trying to get in touch with me. Knowing Bill, I figured he was just putting me on. Then, about two months after my discharge, I got a call one morning from Bill telling me that Stevie Wonder was in town for a performance at Arizona State University's Gammage Auditorium. He asked if Kristi and I wanted to meet him—that very night!

The show was incredible, and after it was over, Bill took us backstage. Now I was impressed, and a little chagrinned, to discover that Bill did, indeed, have a "connection" to Stevie. A few moments later, there he was, Stevie Wonder. I reached out, intending to shake his hand with my standard businessman's handshake. Stevie casually corrected my error, and gave me a big hug. Man, did I ever feel uncool!

As we spoke, it became apparent that he knew my story and who I was. He asked how I was holding up, and the conversation began to move toward a discussion of our faith. Stevie seemed spiritually strong. I could hear the conviction in his voice. We had just begun discussing our beliefs when Stevie was pulled away to meet and greet other fans. But our talk wasn't over. Within just a couple of minutes he returned, and picked up the conversation exactly where we left off. I was really uplifted from knowing that this talented celebrity had taken such a personal interest in my life.

As we were leaving the auditorium that night, I finally admitted to Bill that I had taken umbrage to his assertion of a connection with Stevie Wonder. And at that very moment I flashed on those telephone 'messages' I had assumed were pranks. I guess I should have returned those calls. Nonetheless, I was walking a foot off the ground as we left the arena. I keep a photo of the meeting in my office for that occasional question: "Is that you with Stevie Wonder?"

"Oh, yeah," I casually answer, "Stevie and I are old friends."

Part Four:

"Thou preparest a table before me . . ."

Chapter 19

Rehabilitation:
Arizona Center for the Blind And
Visually Impaired (ACBVI)

During those weeks when I was so fragile and vulnerable in St. Joseph's Hospital, my Mom began to worry how I would function as a blind person in a sighted world. She pored over the yellow pages and found a social service agency called the Arizona Center for the Blind and Visually Impaired (ACBVI). This agency has since become an integral part of my life.

I am so glad that this wonderful group of people was there for me just when I needed them most. I had never heard of the agency before I needed its services. But, I have since learned that it is the only private agency in Maricopa County that provides rehabilitation services to the adult blind and visually impaired. Most surprising to me when I first discovered them, was the fact that they don't charge for many of their services. They are supported almost entirely by grants and donations. Having come from the business sector, I had trouble grasping this "foreign" concept.

When Mom made that first call, she discovered that ACBVI could not initiate their rehabilitation process until I had been released from the hospital.

Mom and I were both frustrated by this because it was clear that the hospital staff was not prepared to deal with a newly blinded patient. Their intentions were good, of course, but they simply didn't have the know-how. As an example, one of the nurses brought in a walking cane for me, but of course it was far too short and much too heavy to be used as a guide cane. The staff also lacked knowledge about how to employ good sighted guide techniques, which caused many difficult and embarrassing moments when they tried to guide me.

As soon as I was released from the hospital, I was eligible to start my intake process at ACBVI, and I signed on immediately. First, Kristi and I had several meetings with a counselor from the center, at which we learned about the services the agency offered, discussed the social ramifications of blindness, and planned for my emotional well being.

Meetings had always been a major part of my life, and as I sat in the counseling meetings, sightless and virtually clueless, I couldn't get over the bizarre feelings I was having about conducting such a dialogue in total darkness. But, once again, there was no doubt that I would be communicating in this way from now on. Then and there I decided that I had better get used to it.

When our counseling sessions were completed, I began my orientation and mobility exercises and my daily living skills training. For the most part, this phase was conducted in and around my home. The orientation and mobility instructor was a wonderful lady, Marnie McCoy. I got to know her very well over our many sessions. Orientation and mobility is a fancy name for learning how to walk with a white cane, interact with a sighted guide, and find your way around a room.

Usually, due to high demand, there is a six-month wait to schedule these training sessions, but because I was one of the few clients on the waiting list willing to brave the desert summer heat, I was able to start my training early. In hindsight, this was a great decision; learning those skills gave me a level of independence, and allowed me to become more comfortable in my new, dark, world.

After teaching me the basic technique of using a white cane, Marnie started taking me on a regular series of long walks around my neighborhood. I would tap myself to curbs and intersections, and cross the road safely. At first, it was really strange and intimidating to walk these familiar, residential streets. What once had been 'safe territory' now seemed like a 'danger zone'. The sidewalks became obstacle courses and the streets became dangerous highways.

I persisted, though, and on days when Marnie wasn't there, I went on walks by myself. My goal was to go on one walk per day, but fear was my constant companion. On many days, I had to force myself to get off of the couch and trek into the darkness, pushing myself to overcome my fear of losing my way home.

I quickly learned that it was important to have a method for identifying my house; I frequently had difficulty finding it. Being totally blind made it tough to find the sidewalk, much less find the house!

My first solution was to take one of our garbage cans and place it on the sidewalk right in front of the house. For several days, this worked great. Then, just as I was gaining a little confidence, a 'helpful' neighbor, unaware of my strategy, decided to do us a favor by returning the can to our back yard while I was out on my walk. It took me 20 minutes to find my house that day.

The trick that worked best—and still does—is to leave a radio playing quietly by my front door. It's never loud enough to annoy the neighbors, but I can hear it from the street, and that serves me well as an audio beacon.

Kristi offered to go on these walks with me, and while I loved the idea of having her as company, I decided that I needed to go it alone, not only for my own sake but also to save her from yet another 'obligation.' One of the pay-offs for my independent attitude was that I eventually gained enough confidence to start taking one of the boys with me in a baby backpack. I'm sure this served as further proof that I still had a head injury, but the boys didn't seem to mind. Usually, the baby would fall asleep during the walk, and I would soon forget he was even there. If the boys had been old enough to know what was going on, maybe they wouldn't have been so relaxed!

Even today, there is no such thing as a casual walk for me. I have to be on constant alert for changes in my environment. I use all of my remaining senses, all of the time. My ears hear even the slightest change in noise level, detect new sounds, and help me interpret such sounds as safe—or not. My cane warns me of obstacles and informs me of changes in the walking surface. Even my feet give me signals about the texture of the surface I am walking on, and my skin tells me the direction of the sun.

As I walk through the world, my brain is constantly at work, calculating, interpreting, and deciding. Oftentimes, I count my steps to gauge distances from point to point. As you can understand, while I'm doing all of this and trying to visualize where I am, projecting my mind to where I'm going, and avoiding any potential obstacles in my path, I can concentrate on nothing but my walking. I don't do well at all with conducting a cell phone conversation when walking alone—and this has turned out to be a bit of a blessing. Now I use my solitary walks as a tool for clearing my mind and focusing on all the things I have to be thankful for.

Perhaps the easiest way for a blind person to get around is to use a sighted guide. The proper way for a sighted person to guide a blind person is for the guide to walk normally, adjusting the pace to the comfort level of his companion. The blind person grasps the guide's elbow and follows along. This allows the guide to have a clear field of vision facing forward. Whenever there's a change approaching, like a curb or a physical obstacle such as a bush or tree trunk, the guide simply announces it and slows down. If the pair needs to navigate a narrow space, the guide moves his elbow back, a sign for the blind person to walk directly behind the guide.

As simple as this technique is, many untrained people try some rather interesting, yet ineffective, methods of guiding the blind. For example, a popular inclination of an untrained sighted guide is to turn around and face the blind person. The guide will then take the person's hand and walk backwards. The obvious problem is that no one is watching where the pair is going. The notion that the guide must, for some unknown reason, watch the person being guided is erroneous.

Learning the sighted guide system helped Kristi and me tremendously. It allowed us to go out in public more easily. It also called less attention to us.

Kristi and I have greatly improved on this skill. We appear to be a fairly normal couple when we are in public now, because I will usually put my arm around her or hold her hand. We just look like another couple that loves to be close.

The cane helped me navigate around the house for the first several months. Eventually, I became familiar enough with the layout to move about easily without it. Kristi is very good at keeping the home clean and free of obstacles, and we've also been fairly successful at teaching the boys to do the same.

In those first days, aside from walks around the block, my mobility was limited. We live in the suburbs, where nothing is close enough to walk to. A popular saying is, "Nobody walks in Phoenix." It's usually too hot here for long walks anyway.

I have considered getting a guide dog, but I'm not really a good candidate. I love dogs, and I understand that they can be very helpful and provide companionship. On the other hand, they require a good deal of maintenance and can be inconvenient at times such as: flying in planes, riding in cars, and going to restaurants.

Getting a guide dog requires a lot of time, too. Most guide schools require a month at their campus for dog assignment and training. It's important to get a dog that you are compatible with and vice versa. Then the two of you are trained how to work with each other. While some people may be able to carve out a month to attend such schools, I never felt I could spare that much time. Between being a father, husband and running a business, I'd be lucky to find a week. A week, I might add, that I'd rather spend on the beach in Mexico with my family.

Another downside of having a guide dog would be getting attached to it and then, sooner or later, having it pass on. I have known a number of people who had dogs that died. Every single one of those people had become very attached to their dog. For some it had not only been a helper, but a constant companion. Without exception, they reported that the loss of their dog was one of the most difficult times of their life. I have decided (at least for now) that I don't want to expose myself to any more grief.

I've heard dogs are great 'chick magnets'. I joke with Kristi that if I were single, I would definitely have a guide dog. Also, if I had to commute any distance by myself, such as attending a university or working in a large office complex, I would get a guide dog.

The truth is, I am very fortunate. Kristi, a family member, a friend, or a co-worker usually takes me to work or to places I need to go. For those times when I can't find anyone to transport me, I have a cab driver, Jim

Lamb. He first chauffeured me years ago, and we've become good friends. I can call him directly, and Jim is dependable and usually available. I've found that taxi services, scheduled through a dispatcher, are often unreliable. Many times I have waited two or three hours for my cab to show. Today, since I am still active in business and quite busy with my charitable activities, that isn't at all acceptable.

But even with all this assistance, getting from place to place is still a major hassle. I am surprised how much I took for granted when I could see. I hopped in my car, went to work, went shopping, worked out, or visited friends, all without a thought. Today, if I want to go anywhere, or do anything, I have to plan how I am going to get there, how long I will be there and who will bring me home. I'm still uncomfortable with depending on other people.

Prior to the accident, I was a very independent person. I drove virtually everywhere by myself and didn't think twice about it. I enjoyed driving and would usually volunteer to drive on long road trips. I can't recall a single time that Kristi drove me anywhere before the accident. I felt that a man's place was behind the wheel. Over the years I have had jobs that required me to drive 60,000 miles a year, and I never minded it at all.

Since I lost my sight, there have been times when I was stranded at work for several hours, couldn't get to the store or been forced to miss events I wanted to attend because I couldn't find a ride. Sometimes, I'm just 'stuck'. And yet, I know that I am in a better position than most people who are blind.

The daily living skills I learned from ACBVI were instrumental in helping me achieve a new but very different state of 'normal'. Instructors from the agency came to my home to teach me how to accomplish everyday tasks such as cooking, cleaning, operating electrical devices, and many other household jobs. I had to re-learn all of the routine chores I had done as a sighted person.

I also needed a way to properly set the controls, so I could use them. The answer was to apply tiny tactile dots—little rubber bumps—to appliances. Sticking these dots on items such as the washer and dryer, dishwasher, microwave oven, and coffee maker have allowed me to use them by 'seeing' with my fingertips.

ACBVI instructors attempted to teach me Braille. Braille is a system of raised dots that allow blind people to read with their fingertips. Many published documents such as books, magazines and instruction manuals are done in Braille. Thanks to the Americans with Disabilities Act, areas in public places such as restrooms, elevators and ATM's are often identified with Braille. (Have you ever noticed that drive-through ATMs often have Braille touch pads? Think about that.)

While learning which dot patterns represented specific letters of the alphabet was not too difficult, I had incredible trouble putting my knowledge into practice when I had to feel with my fingertips and interpret the dot patterns punched into a piece of paper. My perception is that the dots are so close together it's almost impossible to feel the differences. I spent many hours working on this skill with only limited success.

As it turns out, I am not alone. Many adults have the same problem. Some studies indicate that less than 15% of blind adults read Braille. Tactile sensitivity diminishes as one ages. Also, it may be that we 'old dog' adults are less willing to learn 'new tricks.' Most Braille users typically learned the system in childhood.

Nonetheless, I am still very impressed when I am with someone who can read Braille. I am amazed to watch them move their fingers across the page. As far as I am concerned, this skill borders on magic.

Even with my limited Braille skills, though, I still use it to help me out in a number of areas. I certainly won't be reading any novels soon, but I do label items such as files in my office, CD's, flavors of coffee and electronic devices.

In today's world, there are many new methods of getting the printed word to the blind. The books I read are delivered via cassette tape, CD or MP3. I can get virtually any publication; and the quality gets better each year. The people who narrate the books are usually very talented, using various voices for each character. I read a wide variety of books, ranging in topics, from biographies to novels to spiritually inspiring manuscripts. Surprisingly, I read more books now than I did when I could see!

I listen to the newspaper on a special radio developed for the 'print disabled' by Sun Sounds Radio. If I miss it, I can use a dial-up service and access it anytime I want via the telephone. I rarely miss a day; I'm a devoted news junkie.

The Library of Congress makes hundreds of magazines and other publications available to the blind on audiotape at no charge. For example, I receive the Smithsonian magazine and Consumer Reports from them.

I also have the Bible on tape and get various audio taped Bible studies, free of charge. In addition, there are several Internet web sites that allow me to access the Bible for specific books, scriptures, and word studies. I also have a small, digital recorder that has the entire New Testament on it. I can move from chapters and verses with the push of a button.

The real question for me isn't whether or not I can get a given publication in audio form; it is how I can prioritize what I have time to listen to. It does take longer to listen than to read, but I would argue that it can be more enjoyable.

The technology of E-books (files that are formatted as books which can be downloaded into a home computer) is very promising for the blind. Special MP-3 devices have been developed with 'talking' features that make the technology adaptable for people like me.

Most electronic devices available to the general public are digital and require the use of a menu screen. These screens are superfluous for the blind. The older, analog technology was easier to use because it relied on knobs and switches that could be made accessible with the addition of tactile markings.

Of all of the skills I learned from ACBVI, the most important was the adaptive computer technology that allowed me to use the computer with nearly the efficiency of a sighted person. The Center provided me with a software program called JAWS Job Access with Speech. JAWS is a screen-reading program that converts the text on the screen to an automated voice the user can hear. Using the arrow keys and various shortcut keys on my keyboard, I can tell the program what I want to read. Once I had mastered this program I could use Microsoft Word and other word processors and various spreadsheet programs. I can also write and read E-mail and surf the Internet. I have a computerized document scanner that allows me to read letters and other text. I am pleased to say that I'm now an excellent typist and can operate many programs efficiently. Interestingly, I have heard that a blind user can operate a computer 30% faster than a sighted person because the blind person does not have to remove his or her hands from the keyboard to use a mouse.

But getting to this advanced level of proficiency has taken a good deal of time. The first problem I encountered was that I didn't know how to type. I had never learned, because I always relied on a secretary or typing pool to perform this cumbersome task. I had gotten by with the 'hunt and peck' method. When I could no longer 'hunt" I came to the realization that I needed to learn to type.

My lack of this skill became glaringly apparent one day when I wanted to write letters; one to my parents and the other to my staunch supporter and friend Bob Schaefer. I wanted to tell them how much I appreciated all they had done and all they continued to do. In a moment of inspired enthusiasm, I sat down with a yellow pad of paper and a pencil and tried to write the letters. I used a ruler to help me keep my lines straight. I couldn't lift the pencil from the page or I would lose my place.

I managed to get through it, but the letters were nearly illegible and only served to sadden the recipients. Clearly, learning to type would be my ticket out of this dilemma. I also recognized that if I ever wanted to work again, I had to communicate in a more professional manner.

Kristi volunteered to teach me, and we spent many hours cramped in our small home office while she taught me the basics. (If you think installing wallpaper with me was a challenge . . .!) It probably would have been funny if it hadn't been so sad. We were both suffering from serious head injuries, and we were dealing with all of the other complications in our life, including my blindness and our new babies.

Kristi would laboriously show me a block of letters to memorize on the keyboard, and I would confuse them. Frustrated, I would then tell her that she must have told them to me incorrectly, even though she could see the keyboard and I couldn't. This would go on for up to two hours each day. (Are you starting to understand why I think of Kristi as my earth angel?) Luckily, I was absolutely determined to learn this skill because I saw that it would be vitally important for me to communicate via the written word, and Kristi shared that vision, so we hung in there.

Some things, like learning to type, I was able to accomplish with only the help available to me at home and the application of my own will. In other areas, I needed the kind of help that only an organization like ACBVI could offer.

ACBVI has been providing rehabilitation and social recreation programs to the blind and visually impaired community of Maricopa County for over 50 years. They have come a long way—from training blind people to make brooms and tune pianos, (the only jobs available to the blind in the 1950s) to guiding people into careers as attorneys, engineers, doctors and even insurance agents.

The skills I learned at ACBVI gave me the building blocks I needed to proceed with my life as a blind person, both personally and professionally. My gratitude for this was deep and wide, and I wondered how I could ever repay them. Shortly after completing my training at the center, I discovered that they had big payback plans for me!

Chapter 20

Serving ACBVI
As a Board Member

After a year of healing and rehabilitation at ACBVI, I saw a need at the agency. These people had done so much for me, I wanted to return the favor.

As I discovered during my stay at Barrows Neurological Center, there was no agency in Phoenix equipped to assist the newly blind while they were in the hospital convalescing. Those first days of being blind are dark days, a time of unbelievable confusion and desperation. So, I decided some basic training for the staff at Phoenix hospitals would benefit those individuals.

If I had known simple techniques such as proper sighted guide procedures, using the clock method to visualize food on a plate, and how to be able to tell the difference between day and night with a talking watch, my first days as a blind man would have been much easier.

I left a message with Jim LaMay, the Executive Director at ACBVI. I offered to serve as a 'first contact' for the agency to help patients who'd just become blind. Even though I wasn't trained as a blind skills instructor, I believed that I could pass along some helpful hints straight from my own experience.

The next day, Jim called and asked if we could get together to discuss the project. I was thrilled, and we made an appointment. I had but a single purpose in mind, but Jim envisioned loftier goals.

Jim quickly approved my concept. He then said that he had another matter to discuss with me, an idea that hit me with impressive force. He asked if I would be interested in joining the Board of Directors for the agency. I was taken totally by surprise, but I was flattered that he would ask. It didn't take me more than a few seconds to 'get' that it really made a lot of sense: I could bring my business acumen to the Board but, more importantly, because I was blind, I would be a flesh-and-blood representative of our client base.

I discussed Jim's offer with Kristi, who thought it was a great idea. The next day I agreed to join the Board. It wasn't long before I began to joke that I had become the "poster boy" for the agency.

At that time, I had no concept of the huge role this agency would play in my life.

My membership on the Board definitely helped me to build my confidence and sense of self-worth, which had been lagging since the accident. The fact that an agency like ACBVI trusted me enough to help them make important decisions regarding the agency's operations had a positive impact on me.

After I served for two years as a Board member, I was asked to become the President. I served in that position for four years, a time during which I helped to guide the agency through many exciting changes.

In 2001, we embarked on a $1,000,000 remodeling project at our main facility. The building had not been touched in 30 years, and it showed. How bad was it? I began telling people that I thought it looked like a dump—and I couldn't even see it!

Before the remodeling project, the center was housed in two separate buildings and at three different locations on the property. Growth had been sporadic and ill-planned, occurring incrementally over the prior three decades. In a physical sense, it was difficult for a sighted person—much less for blind people—to figure out where they were going.

After one Board meeting, a woman who was also blind asked me to guide her back to the main office. I guess she figured I had a cane, so I must know where I was going. Well, I got us to the middle of an adjacent parking lot, finally having to admit to her that I was a bit lost. She wisely decided to let someone else take over! That was the last time she asked for my assistance—on anything.

After a frustrating meeting at which one of the wheels on my chair collapsed, nearly toppling me to the floor, I made a personal vow. Something had to be done about the decrepit condition of the facility, and I was the one to do it. I thought back to the elegant offices I'd seen in the corporate world and how unfair it was. After all, the services we were providing were much more important and beneficial to the community than those of a corporation whose main objective was to make money for its shareholders.

I had no idea how we were going to achieve the lofty goal of a complete remodel, but I knew it had to be done. I relied on the adage, "It's not what you know, it's *who* you know." This philosophy for getting things done had served me well over the years.

Bob Schaefer, who was also on the ACBVI Board, recruited personal friend and client, Jack Wilmeng, who owned a commercial construction company. After touring our dilapidated facility, Jack not only agreed to join our Board, but to also serve as our construction expert. He eventually took on the remodeling project, providing his services as a contribution to the agency and saving us untold amounts of money by selecting subcontractors who would work for us on the slimmest of profit margins. (Some didn't charge for anything but materials!) Jack also convinced architect Bob Winton to donate his services. (Sadly, Jack passed away in 2005. We will forever be grateful for what he provided for ACBVI).

Over time, we were able to build our Board with some "can do" individuals from the community. I even got my sister Janice involved. Propelled by a successful capital needs campaign and the good fortune of receiving some large grants, we were able to fund the project.

After months of planning and design work, we developed a blueprint for our new agency's home. We included the entire staff in the decision making process. After all, who could better know the unique and special needs of our clients? We gave much consideration to making the Center more accessible for the clients. Thus, items such as unique floor coverings and textures, contrasting wall colors and surfaces, handrails, special lighting, and Braille signage were incorporated into the final plans.

We designed the facility to showcase our adaptive computer technology center. We located that department in the central core of the building, surrounding it with large interior windows so that visitors could easily see into the room. This state-of-the-art operation caters to many different disabilities, not just to the blind and visually impaired. Many of the agency's clients are quadriplegics and/or hearing impaired. With the help of some amazing devices, these clients can often run circles around sighted computer users.

The arts and crafts center was expanded and completely updated, and areas such as our demonstration kitchen and counseling offices were also enlarged and remodeled. In the new, larger space, we were now able to have a client library, a low-vision center and a conference room with enough space to accommodate our entire Board, which had been difficult, indeed, in our old facility with its cramped spaces and small conference rooms. To my delight, the wheels of our brand-new boardroom chairs were permanently attached—and they still are.

Perhaps our most significant improvement was the fact that the entire operation was now housed under one roof at 3150 E. Roosevelt in Phoenix. We are extremely proud of our facility and look for any opportunity to show it off.

When I rotated off the Board in 2001, Kristi and I were honored with a mural to recognize us for our contributions to ACBVI. (So much for not announcing our good works with trumpets)!

The piece is a large, three-dimensional collage entitled "Pathways to Independence." The theme is: how one can obtain skills and confidence to succeed in the world in spite of his or her disabilities. The artists, Helen Helwig and Niki Glen, also incorporated work that was created by clients of ACBVI. And because it is tactile, blind people can 'see' it.

Kristi and I were overwhelmed at the unveiling ceremony. We felt a bit uncomfortable receiving the accolades. On a personal note, I honestly feel I have gotten more from the agency than I have given.

I took a one-year sabbatical from the Board, but in 2003 I rejoined and am once again serving as the President. I continue to be excited about the future of this outstanding organization.

Chapter 21

The Welker Invitational Golf Tournament

Shortly after the accident, some friends of ours decided to hold a golf tournament and auction to help Kristi and me defray some of our medical expenses. In August of 1994, Dino Paul, Dave Robertson and Bob Schaefer got together to put on the first annual Welker Invitational golf tournament and auction.

On a hot August afternoon, we gathered for the fundraiser at Club West Golf Course, in the foothills of Phoenix. In later years, Bob confessed that he and Dave had previously spoken about developing a golf tournament. He jokingly thanked me for providing them with a cause to do just that.

The first year's tournament was a very emotional time for Kristi and me. It had been less than four months since the accident, and I had been home for just a few weeks. We were both suffering from head injuries, a tremendous amount of stress, and I had limited stamina. To cap it all off, this was the first time a lot of our friends and colleagues had seen us since the accident—the first time they had seen me as a blind person. I can understand why they might have been uncomfortable. The concept of having a friend, who was sighted one day and blind the next, must have been difficult.

During the day, we spent only an hour at the tournament, and it was a major ordeal. We brought our babies with us so we could show them off. After getting Kristi and the boys settled in the clubhouse, Chris Hahn and I climbed into a cart and set off to visit some of the golfers.

The fairways were lined with individuals who were here for the sole purpose of helping Kristi and me. It was overwhelming. There were family, friends, business colleagues, people we barely knew, and people we didn't know at all. Some of the golfers had flown in from various parts of the country. With all of this external input invading my remaining senses, it wasn't long before the emotion and the heat soon caught up with me and we had to go home to rest.

Kristi and I returned that night for the dinner and auction, and again we tried to put on our best faces. It was important to thank everyone for their support, so I had spent much of the afternoon trying to put my thoughts into words. It was, by far, the most difficult speech I had ever made, but I wanted to convey that we were going to be OK, and I also wanted to stress the importance of *not ever taking life for granted*.

Bob Schaefer introduced me, and when the applause died out and I began to speak, it became uncomfortably quiet in the room, so quiet that I couldn't help wondering whether everyone had left the building. But I forged on and was soon rewarded by more applause—and even laughter at a joke I shared. After I had thanked everyone as best I could, I quickly moved on to the "don't take it for granted" part. Here is a bit of what I said.

"Don't take for granted the ability to look into your partner's beautiful eyes, to watch your babies smile, or to see their little hands wrap around your finger. Don't take for granted your ability to move freely about your house or your neighborhood, or to jump into your car for a trip to the store. Don't take for granted your ability to play sports such as basketball, even if you are on a bad team. Don't take for granted your ability to sit down and read the Sunday paper or to read a good novel— or a bad one, for that matter. Simply put: embrace every precious moment."

Not a very lighthearted speech, I know. But it did surprise me that when I finished, it was nearly as quiet as when I started. In 10 minutes, I had managed to turn a festive occasion into a rather somber—or at least reflective—one.

Rising to thank me for my message, Bob immediately lightened the mood by telling everyone it was the last time he would let me speak at my own tournament. Even I laughed at that, but I knew and felt the truth of what I had said, and many people have reminded me of how deeply it affected them.

The highlight of the evening was a live auction. The most popular item in the auction was an autographed Kevin Johnson game jersey—with his connections, Dr. Holcombe was always able to get us great Phoenix Suns and Arizona Diamondbacks memorabilia. Thanks to my recent visit with KJ and the support he had provided me, I really wanted this jersey. Unfortunately, Phoenix Suns memorabilia, especially KJ stuff, was very popular at the time and the bidding quickly got too rich for my blood and I dropped out. I may have been the guest of honor, but this was sports memorabilia business! As the bidding on the jersey ended, I was surprised at how much the item had brought. I was even more surprised to discover the winning bidder was Don Mayer, a friend and business associate from Salt Lake City. At the end of the evening, as buyers came to pick up the items they had won, Don shocked me by giving me the jersey as a gift. It now hangs in my office along with some other items KJ gave me, and it's one of my most prized possessions, not only because it's a KJ original, but also because it was given to me by a true friend.

The Welker Charity Tournament became an annual event. During its ten-year run, we donated over $240,000 to the Arizona Center for the Blind and Visually Impaired (ACBVI). It was a great event and I will always be thankful to all of the golfers, donors and volunteers who contributed their time and talents to this worthwhile cause. I looked forward to it every year and was always amazed at the support we received.

Starting in the second year, my official duty during the tournament was to man the "Blind Golfer Charity Hole." My sister Janice, brother-in-law Joe, my niece Tawnya, and I would select a par four hole with wide fairways and set up camp at the tees. As each foursome came through, we would solicit a donation. In return for the donation, I would hit the group's drive for them. The bonus was that, regardless of where the drive ended up, the group would be lying zero. Sometimes they would have a chip shot to the green. At other times, however, there would be quite a bit of work left. It really didn't matter where they ended up. The important thing was that it raised more money for the charity.

I really enjoyed the Charity Hole because it gave me a chance to personally visit with each of the golfers and thank them for their participation. It also gave the golfers a chance to see that, with a little luck, a blind guy could hit the ball pretty well.

I would have to say the highlight of the Charity Hole was the year I out-hit Bob Schaefer on his drive. I'm sure I had a little help from above that day, but I never let him forget that for as long as he lived.

Pat McGroder, who has helped me in so many other ways, as well, was a principal supporter of the tournament from the very beginning. One year he underwrote the cost of the entire tournament. We later hosted the event at his Scottsdale Golf Course, Silverado Golf Club. Pat is known in the Valley of the Sun as someone who gives back to the community, and he certainly did that for us.

My niece, Tawnya Sauer, has recently taken the helm of our organization and is energetically moving in new directions. Updating the events to salsa dance competitions and beep ball tournaments (softball for the blind), I am confident she can continue the great work of fund raising for at least another ten years.

Chapter 22

Returning to Work

It took me an entire year at home, recovering and learning how to function as a blind person, before I figured out two things: The first was the realization that staying home taking care of babies was a lot more demanding than I would have thought; the second was that I wanted to go back to work, whatever that would look like.

It really surprised me to realize how much of my self-worth I'd put into my career. I never understood how important work was for my well-being until I was unable to do it. Going to work gave me a feeling of accomplishment, affirming for me that I was really doing something worthwhile in the world. During most of that first year of my "new life" I was really down; I felt that I was no longer a productive member of society.

Prior to the accident, I had been working as a commercial property and casualty insurance agent at Schaefer/Smith/Ankeney (SSA), a large broker in Phoenix. I had been there only six months but had realized some early successes and was beginning to feel pleased with my auspicious start.

Before I joined SSA, I had spent the previous 11 years working for two insurance carriers, Westfield Insurance and Transamerica Insurance—on the "company side" of the industry. For those two firms I had worked as a commercial lines property and casualty underwriter and, for about five years, as a field marketing representative. While I really enjoyed those positions, I wasn't overjoyed with the vagaries of corporate life, and eventually concluded that my company days were numbered. The problem with the corporate career path, in my opinion, was that if I wanted to move up the company ladder, I would have to travel extensively and relocate frequently. The idea of packing up my wife and sons and moving across the country every few years at the company's whim wasn't acceptable to me. I wasn't single any more, and Kristi and I had decided Phoenix was our home. I would also have to continue dealing with the inevitable company hierarchy and the politics that came with it. In addition, unless I reached the upper level of corporate management, my income potential would always be limited.

By making the jump to the agency side—the "retail" side of the insurance business—I was assured that I wouldn't have to transfer to another city. I would also self-determine my own future both in terms of the work I would do and the income I could earn. The downside was that, if I didn't build my own book of business, I would eventually be forced to return to the company side.

Notice how I have referred to the "company side" and the "agency side." This is because these two components of the industry seem to be at battle most of the time—their primary goals are diametrically opposed. The insurance companies are looking to cover businesses that incur few or no claims, while agents are looking to write as much business as possible to increase their commissions, irrespective of the potential risks involved.

This is, of course, an oversimplification of a very complex relationship between companies, agents and their clients, but it is a major factor in the strategies that each employ.

It is difficult to make the move from company to agency, or vice versa, and few individuals make it successfully. I think the reason I was starting off so well was that I had spent the first four years of my career working on the agency side with my Dad and brother. I had no misperceptions of what to expect. I also think that my agency experience served me well during my company days. I was able to relate to the agents better than most, and I worked from the premise that neither the agents nor the company people were the "bad guys."

Soon after joining SSA I decided to specialize in two fields: petroleum marketers and high tech manufacturers. I educated myself to the unique needs of these industries in regards to loss exposure, and I studied the critical and unique coverages they required. I attended seminars and conventions and sought insurance companies with the best programs, services and pricing for each. I felt that to be successful I had to become an expert in a specific field.

Adjusting to the agency side, especially SSA, was very interesting and consistently exciting. I was already familiar with the agency because I had called on them for five years as a marketing representative for both Westfield and Transamerica. One of my best friends, Bob Schaefer, was the son of one of the agency's owners (Bill Schaefer), and he was a successful producer. From the very first day, I felt at home.

After the accident, the owners and staff of SSA were absolutely amazing. They couldn't have been more caring and supportive. I could never have anticipated what was going to happen in our life. It was clear to Kristi and me that my choice to join this firm had been a wise one.

Bob Schaefer and his wife Courtney quickly stepped up and took over all of our financial duties after the accident. Kristi designated Courtney as the holder of our power of attorney. They were there for us every hour of every day. As I mentioned earlier, Bob came to visit me constantly in the hospital. It seemed as though he was by my side at all times. His Dad, Bill, phoned me almost daily with words of encouragement and support. While the thought of going back to work was the furthest thing from my mind at that time, their personal contact gave me increased conviction and an elevated level of confidence that I would overcome my disability.

One day, Bob visited and brought along another of the agency's owners, Jim Hartman. Toward the end of our time together, Bob (impulsively, it turned out) blurted out that they would hold my office for me in case I ever wanted to return. There was a 'pregnant pause', and then Jim agreed with Bob's commitment. Bob laughed about this later because he didn't really have the authority to make such a promise. He did believe, however, that the agency principals would back him up, which they did. My office sat dark, despite the fact that the agency was overcrowded. A year after the accident that had nearly cost me my life and had taken my sight, I decided I wanted to return to work, determined to succeed. I was buoyed by the knowledge that the agency, which couldn't have been more accommodating, was offering me a hand-up, not a hand-out.

Did I worry about whether or not I could function successfully as a blind insurance agent? Of course I did! I was a neophyte to this disability and had no idea what a blind person was capable of, but with a little help, I got some answers.

Lanny Hair, a long-time friend and the Executive Vice President of the state insurance agents' trade association, the Independent Insurance Agents & Brokers of Arizona, contacted his counterparts throughout the country, asking if they knew of any agents who were blind. He then provided me with a list of several successful blind agents.

I contacted the agents from Lanny's list and was encouraged by their favorable attitude about the infinite possibilities. In each interview, I tried to discover the secrets of how they accomplished their jobs and what methods they used to overcome their disabilities. One strong impression I got was that these guys sounded like businessmen, not disabled people. I thought to myself, if they can do it, so can I. I marshaled the will and the courage to go back to work.

The day of my move-in was particularly tough. Everything from my old office had been packed, and as I took things out of their boxes I was reminded time and again of the life I had left behind. My old files, books, and manuals were simply things I could no longer see. And all of the personal memorabilia took me back to my world just before the accident.

One of the interesting changes I discovered upon my return was that my personal office had been moved. It was larger—and it had a big window! Oh well, it was a nice thought.

My first day back at work was very emotional for everybody. It was the first time most of my co-workers had seen me since I left on that Friday afternoon almost exactly a year before. I was now totally blind and needed an all-too-visible white cane to get around the office. Fortunately, I knew the layout and could rely on my memory to orient myself most of the time. As I moved through the office, I began to notice an interesting phenomenon. For the first few days, as I entered a new work area, I heard all conversation come to an abrupt halt. The silence was deafening. I am sure the sight of me fumbling my way around was a little disturbing and sad for most, but within a few days I had become just another colleague, and eventually, the office was noisy all the time again, even when I passed by.

In order to facilitate my return to work, SSA offered to purchase all of the adaptive computer equipment I would need. They did this, I might add, without the requirements of the Americans with Disabilities Act (ADA). I was no longer capable of doing the job I was hired to do. I believe they could have terminated me with no problems. Instead, they created an inside position in the commercial lines small accounts department.

Although I could no longer work with the large processing and manufacturing risk I had been working with prior to the accident, I was more than qualified to handle smaller, vanilla clients. Larger risks are typically more complex and require physical inspections, research of existing coverages and in depth analysis of insurance exposures. These clients demand a lot of personal attention and frequent visits. These were all duties I could no longer realistically perform.

Most small accounts, on the other hand, could be handled successfully using only the telephone, fax and e-mail. They didn't require personal visits or the expertise and oversight of larger-risk clients. Working in the small account unit was something I thought I could easily handle. I did, after all, have a college degree in insurance, was a certified insurance counselor and had been in the business for over fifteen years.

My computer was equipped with a screen reader so I could navigate the special insurance program software, my calendar, phone numbers, addresses, e-mail and the Internet. There was also a scanner so I could read letters and other pertinent documents.

It takes me and my screen reader somewhat longer to accomplish tasks than it does for a sighted person. That being said, it is truly amazing what adaptive computer technology can do for the blind. This technology has leveled the playing field and allowed me to return to work, and it keeps getting better. One of my more interesting "cheaters" was a specialized telephone headset that allowed me to listen to my talking computer in one ear and the person I was talking to in the other. The specially configured sweep microphone on this headset left my hands free for typing. The person I was talking to was never aware of my screen reader "feeding" me information in my other ear. I could also tape record calls to capture detailed information I needed later. Most clients had no idea I was blind, and that was my goal.

As for how they treated me, my fellow employees fell into the same basic three categories as the people I encountered elsewhere in my new life.

The first category was the "head for the exits" group. These folks couldn't handle or accept me with my new disability. They couldn't get over the fact that I was now blind. They were nervous and were unable to maintain a normal conversation. Many of them simply dropped out of my life, which was probably better for both them and me. They were uncomfortable, which made me uncomfortable, too.

The abandonment of these people, some of whom I considered close friends, was one of the most surprising and disappointing developments to come out of the tragedy. The fact that these folks could not accept me as a blind person was simply inconceivable to me. Here, at my time of need, the moments at which I could have greatly benefited from their support and encouragement, they turned their backs. I rationalized that, if these folks only wanted me as a friend when I was 'normal', they were not true friends anyway. Regardless of my logical rationalization, it still hurt. I finally had to take the position that their inability to accept me was their problem, not mine.

The second group of people I call the "over-functioners." These are the folks who want to help so much that they rush to take over every conceivable task. They think I am no longer capable of doing even the simplest things, such as ordering at a restaurant or closing a car door. This is the group that will inevitably twist open the cap on a bottle of water before handing it to me, like I can't possibly figure out how to do it myself. They often worry that I will unexpectedly fall down without warning when we are walking, so they hold onto my arm to keep me up. I can work with this group. Their hearts are in the right place, and, given a little time, they can figure out what I can and cannot do.

The final group is the "so you're blind, let's move on" group. These are the individuals who accept my blindness and realize that inside I am still Steve Welker. They understand that I am the same person and my intelligence level has remained the same. These are the people I am most comfortable with, and they are the people who have helped me accomplish much of what I have so far.

One of the individuals in the last category was Ben Greer. He'd been a producer for the agency and a friend of mine for several years. When I started at the agency, Ben took me under his wing and showed me the ropes of retail business insurance. He was an honest, hard working agent, and I learned a lot from him.

One day, Ben walked into my office and sat down. After a couple of minutes of pleasantries, Ben told me he had a friend who had been in a serious auto accident and had also suffered head injuries. He told me that his injured friend now seemed a little goofy in the head, but that I did not appear to suffer from the same affliction. (Thanks for the vote of confidence, Ben! You don't seem goofy in the head, either). But that conversation, as unusual as it was, helped me to once again realize how fortunate I was.

As the months passed, I became more and more comfortable in the workplace. Most of the people around me became more comfortable, too. I began to sell and service accounts again, and I felt increasingly productive. I began to enjoy the work, the people, even the mechanics of getting the job done. I began to believe that I could actually pull this off as a blind person.

Later that year, I was asked to present an award at the annual Independent Insurance Agents and Brokers state convention. It was a "coming out" appearance of sorts and proved very memorable.

The previous year's convention was held a couple of months after my accident, and they named an award in my honor. To the best of my knowledge, these awards were only given posthumously. Joe Bensfeld, a good friend, was the President of the association that year, which probably accounts for why the award was named in my honor—I think he figured I wouldn't make it! At any rate, the award is given to the industry associate of the year, and I had won it in 1988. When it came time for the presentation, I stepped up to the lectern and, before introducing the winner, I apologized for surviving my accident. But I did it with humor, moving right on to the presentation itself. Afterwards, a colleague came up and thanked me for not using the old Mark Twain quote, "Rumors of my demise have been greatly exaggerated." To this day, the association still calls it the Steve Welker award. I think the whole thing is kind of amusing. At the same time, I am humbled by the gesture of recognition by my peers.

Getting out of the house was an important part of the process, as well. Here's the truth of that. I enjoyed being home with the family, but going to work gave me a sense of accomplishment and purpose I needed in order to flourish. It was proof to me that, at least for us men, self-confidence can be directly tied to career success.

In my case, I was no longer just sitting around the house day after day; I was out there, going to work! We don't talk about this subject much, but I'm sure my re-entry into the working world helped Kristi as well.

Returning to the workplace was therapeutic in other ways, too. I appreciated the everyday occurrences I had previously taken for granted. The back-and-forth camaraderie with co-workers, going to lunch, even attending meetings—every little thing took on new, expanded, brighter meaning, and from time to time I experienced moments of real enjoyment.

The lesson here for me was simple; going back to work improved my sense of well being more than any medication or therapy could have ever done. I was back in the saddle, I had done it!

Chapter 23

Opening My Own Insurance Agency

A fter working at Schaefer/Smith/Ankeney for a year, I felt I needed more of a challenge. While working with the smaller accounts provided me with the foothold I needed to get myself back into the workplace, I wanted (and needed) to do more.

It was at this time I decided to open my own insurance agency. It would be a full service commercial lines agency. I would start from scratch. I didn't do this to prove anything to anybody but myself. I had to do this to prove that I was capable of running my own business.

I have made a lot of friends and acquaintants in the insurance community over the years, which made this start-up work.

There is an adage I like that says, "In life, you meet the same people on your way down the ladder that you met on your way up. How they treat you on the way down is directly related to how you treated them on the way up."

I guess I must have done something right because they were certainly there for me when I needed them. For instance, the relationships I had with various carriers and brokers provided me with the agency appointments I needed. Appointments are generally tough to get in this industry and I was fortunate to have them. Craig Hedrick, a branch manager I worked for at Transamerica Insurance and was now at CBIC, took a chance and provided me with an important appointment without hesitation. Such an appointment for a start-up agency with no book of business is virtually unheard of. I will never forget the trust Craig gave me.

My relationships with other insurance agents were a tremendous help as well. I relied heavily on Don Mayer of Salt Lake City, Utah, and Doug Carr and Armando Miranda of Mesa, Arizona. These guys were there for me to bounce ideas off of, provide expertise and help secure markets for my clients. Without them and many others, I don't think I would have been able to pull it off.

The first logical step in starting my agency was to secure an office manager, but I really needed much more than that. I needed a person who could not only work the insurance desk but could also handle claims, bookkeeping and all of the other administrative duties required in a small office. I also needed someone to help select office space, purchase furniture and set up the office with me.

In addition, this person had to fall into my "people category three," the "so you're blind, let's move on" group. I needed someone who recognized my capabilities, not my limitations, someone who would take a chance with their career on this high-risk proposition.

I was fortunate to find such a person in a friend I had worked with at Transamerica Insurance. Kim Noetzel and I had kept in touch over the years, and she was a huge help to Kristi and me after the accident, so she was very aware of my current limitations and capabilities.

For the most part, opening the agency was exciting. Designing the layout, advertising, choosing furniture and equipment, selecting a name and logo—I enjoyed the whole process. Even the mundane tasks like setting-up the phone service and hooking up the electricity gave me a sense of accomplishment. Being responsible for virtually every aspect of the decision making process was going to be rewarding, indeed.

The business got off to a slow start and we worked hard. Month by month and year by year we eventually built the book of business that sustained us. We found creative ways to work around my disability and make it as seamless as possible.

Most times, prospective clients were not aware I was blind until we showed up to do the proposals. I would typically gather all of the underwriting information I needed via phone, fax and e-mail. Kim and I worked as a team, doing the presentation and conducting a perfectly normal business transaction.

I don't believe my blindness ever negatively affected an opportunity to land an account. While a prospect may have initially been somewhat uncomfortable with the situation, I think that my knowledge and professionalism quickly eased any concerns. On some occasions, in fact, I know that my disability worked in my favor. After all, who wouldn't trust a blind insurance agent?

My parents played an important role in my new agency, too. On the business side, they wanted an office in Phoenix to market Mexican auto insurance. They sub-let some space from me. In addition, I helped them place business insurance from their Ajo, Bisbee and Douglas offices.

The most important support I received from them was more practical. They were always there for me, to discuss various problems that inevitably came up, to provide suggestions from their experience, or just go to lunch. We always ate lunch at IHOP. We joked that IHOP was our official corporate lunchroom.

An interesting thing developed as we grew our book of business. Most of the agents and brokers I competed with had minimum commission levels at which they would pay their producers. It follows, then, that most agents would look for easy-to-place and larger business cases and were reluctant to work with smaller, harder-to-place ones. For this reason, there were not many qualified agents helping small businesses with their insurance. High-risk, hard-to-place small businesses had a difficult time finding an agent who would invest the time and knowledge required to locate carriers. We often decided to take on such businesses, and as a result, had a disproportionately high percentage of small, high-risk clients. This was fine with me; I liked working on challenges more than on the vanilla accounts.

One of my best clients turned out to be my friend and personal attorney, Patrick McGroder. Soon after I opened the agency, he told me he wanted me to be his agent. I handled his personal insurance, his office, his golf course and, yes, even his muscle car collection I remembered on that first day we met in the hospital.

Most importantly, of course, was that Pat trusted me and had unending confidence in my ability to serve as his insurance agent. Pat is a definitely a high-profile individual in the Phoenix business community, and handling his insurance was a real feather in my cap.

Running a successful insurance agency brought great rewards almost every day. It was hard work at times, but I loved the challenge. Putting together insurance programs, helping businesses with their insurance needs, and working with company underwriters gave me the sense that what I was doing was important, that I was contributing to the business world and making a difference.

After we had been operating for about three years, my brother Jim joined the agency. We had previously worked together at my Dad's agency, but Jim had moved to the grocery business. Eventually, though, he tired of the hard work and long hours. After joining us, he discovered that insurance work was mentally difficult, but at least the hours were better and there was no heavy lifting.

The time I spent working with Jim was great. He's nine years older than me, so we never had the traditional older/younger brother relationship. Given the significant difference in our ages, our interests had never been alike, so this time together finally gave us an opportunity to get to know each other better.

Because most of my clients were small business owners, I had the opportunity to see first hand just how hard the majority of them worked. Being blind made my business endeavor more difficult in some ways, but I never felt that my disability got in the way of my productivity.

Owning and operating a business is certainly more demanding than most people realize, and insurance is particularly so because the product is intangible and the service aspect is extremely time consuming. In my case, I made that point by telling folks I was the hardest working man in the insurance business. I would tell them, "It's dark when I go to work in the morning and dark when I come home at night!"

In the summer of 2004, I sold my business to Garrett Hatch, the principal of Hatch Insurance Agency. I had worked with Garrett for several years, and our approach to the business was compatible. I trusted him, which was most important. My clients were like family to me, so I wanted to make sure that they would be taken care of.

After owning and operating my insurance agency successfully for nine years, I decided it was time to move to the next stage of my life. The insurance field had been very good to me and I had no complaints. I met a lot of great people, the industry had proven relatively stable over the years and, boring as it sounds, I found it interesting.

That being said, it was time to move in a completely different direction. Today, while still an insurance consultant, I concentrate the majority of my time and energy to serving the Arizona Center for the Blind and Visually Impaired as the President of the Board of Directors, conducting motivational speaking, and writing. I feel that my story may help others make positive changes in their own lives and help them overcome their own tragedies.

Chapter 24

The United Way

One of the positive things to come out of my tragedy has been my involvement with the United Way. I am honored to be a volunteer spokesperson for this outstanding organization. But it was quite a fluke that got me started in this role.

The Arizona Center for the Blind and Visually Impaired (ACBVI), the agency that helped me with my rehabilitation, receives a good deal of its annual funding from the Valley of the Sun United Way. Once a year, the United Way sends out an allocations panel to visit ACBVI to verify that the agency is still worthy of funding.

Shortly after I joined the Board of Directors at ACBVI, Jim LaMay, the Executive Director, asked me to make a presentation at the annual allocation panel meeting. He wanted me to share my personal story as an example of how their services had helped me put my life back together. I was excited by this opportunity and agreed right away. I was eager to share my experiences in any way that might help the agency. I had already shared my story with the nation on the Leeza Gibbons show, so it wasn't exactly a secret.

After the meeting, a representative from the United Way introduced herself and asked if I would be interested in sharing my story at one of their training sessions. Feeling a bit flattered, I told her I would and that I hoped it would be helpful.

After that first training session, I was hooked. The room was packed. I was a little anxious, but I couldn't see the people (that would have made me really nervous) and I had a story to tell, so off I went. They listened intently and laughed at most of my jokes and when I finished, I received something that I had never experienced as an insurance agent—a standing ovation. What I learned was that it's the story, not the speaker that has an impact. A woman came up afterwards to thank me. She said that my story made her laugh and cry, a comment I've heard many times since that first speech. I realize that what makes the story so appealing is that I'm an average guy who has overcome a horrific event and has managed to keep my sense of humor—and that's what I share and how I share it.

After those training sessions were completed, United Way asked me to become a spokesperson for them, sharing my story with employees from various companies, showing them, in a way, how their donations benefit others. In my story, my example is ACBVI, which assists thousands of individuals like me and is only one of hundreds of 'helping' agencies the United Way supports in the Phoenix area.

Many times, I think my story scares some people. Let's face it. An accident like mine could happen to anyone, so I find that many men in my demographic group—male, 30 to 50 years old, white-collar professionals—increase their pledges significantly after I speak to them. I'm told that they (and many others, if the truth be told) get really serious and introspective when I urge them to contribute generously. I think there's no doubt that my story hits them a little harder than most.

Over the years, I have done hundreds of presentations for the United Way. I have spoken to local organizations, to Fortune 500 companies, and everything in between. I have presented to laborers, managers and CEOs. I have also spoken at Arizona State University, at several Phoenix area hospitals, and before a number of city, county and state governmental agencies. I've been honored to speak to the Tocqueville society, an elite group of philanthropic leaders who have each donated over $10,000 to the United Way. At a special event held at former Senator Barry Goldwater's home in 2006, I thanked the group for giving over $6.6 million during the previous campaign.

Kristi, Colton, Dylan and I have appeared in United Way commercials, print ads and promotional videos. Over the years, I have done radio interviews and public service announcements, too. At times, it felt like we were The United Way poster family. We have certainly enjoyed our relationship with this special organization.

While I have appreciated every speaking opportunity, from the plant workers at Honeywell, to the executives at American Express, some of my favorites are the talks I have given to professional sports teams. I have been privileged to make presentations to teams like the Phoenix Suns, Arizona Diamondbacks, Arizona Cardinals and Phoenix Coyotes.

One I'll never forget was a presentation to the Phoenix Suns in 1997 at America West Arena. When we arrived, Kristi and I were escorted to the executive offices to meet with Jerry Colangelo, CEO and General Manager of the team. The late Cotton Fitzsimmons, the former Suns coach who was assisting Jerry at the time, was there ahead of us. For me, this was very exciting. I had been a Suns fan since 1968, their first season. A lot of my childhood heroes played for the Suns.

Jerry and Cotton were very friendly. Jerry was deeply involved with the United Way. In fact, he and I had previously done a couple of presentations together. I had also met Cotton at a prior event, and I had talked with him when I visited the Suns locker room during a game. After we visited for a few minutes, they led us back to that locker room. At that time, Kevin Johnson (KJ) was still playing for the Suns. When I finished my presentation, we got to catch-up with him a little bit. Kevin hadn't seen me since his visit at St. Joseph's Hospital over three years before. He commented that I had come a long way. In truth, he probably thought I was never going to leave that hospital.

We brought a camera, hoping to get our picture taken with some of the Suns players, but before we could ask, Kevin grabbed the camera from Kristi and started asking some of the guys to pose with us while he took the pictures. I now have those photos hanging in my office. It was all very impressive.

Another memorable presentation was to the staff and coaches of the Arizona Diamondbacks at Bank One Ballpark in 2004. I did the speech from the top of the first base dugout while the audience sat in the first few sections. Kristi and I took Colton and Dylan out of school that day so they could attend. Both boys are huge Diamondback fans, and I won major brownie points with the boys that day. I was no longer just their boring Dad. I was famous! Mark Grace, the former Arizona Diamondback and Chicago Cub standout, hosted the event. He was a good guy and great with the boys. He played catch with them and signed autographs. After the meeting, the Diamondbacks trainer, Paul Lessard, took us down to the locker room for a tour, which impressed the boys mightily. When we took them back to school, they proudly displayed the new wristbands they had received which read "United We Play," the Diamondbacks United Way slogan. For the rest of that day at school, they proudly told anyone who would listen where they got them.

Another interesting thing happened after that meeting. A man introduced himself to me as a member of the medical staff at the ballpark, but, he told me, he had previously served as an emergency medical technician for helicopter rescue and had come on shift just a few hours after our accident. He told me that the EMT's who tended to me at the scene and flew me to the hospital didn't think I was going to make it.

As he sat in the audience and listened to me tell the details of the accident, he had put the pieces together. He said that listening to me made him proud of the services EMT's provide. Usually, they get to see victims only at the accident scene, he said, and seeing me standing there full of life, telling my story, joking around and giving back to the community put a smile on his face. That conversation put a tear in my eye and I remember thinking that there were so many EMT's, police officers, firemen, doctors, nurses and various other medical personnel I never had the chance to thank for saving my life. Perhaps my work with the United Way is how I'm making my payback. And, at the same time, those opportunities to share my story have helped me in my healing process. Ironic, isn't it? Those incredible medical teams are still contributing to me even as I make a contribution to them.

These years of experience making United Way presentations have also helped me to sharpen my public speaking skills. I have branched out and now speak to a diverse group of associations, churches, social agencies, schools and youth organizations, to name a few. I jokingly refer to myself as the reluctant ambassador for the blind. While the message varies slightly from group to group, the underlying theme is the same—with the help of the good Lord above, the community, family and friends; it is possible to overcome incredible odds.

Chapter 25

Losing Our Home To Toxic Mold

S ome people think that any one person shouldn't have to endure more than one major tragedy in their life. They rationalize that if someone has already suffered one maelstrom, they don't deserve any more. This is, of course, an erroneous assumption, one I've never bought into. While some people seem to go through life never having to face major obstacles, it is certainly not the case for the majority of us. For this reason, I've never felt immune to the possibility of another crisis in my life. And that's a good thing.

After returning home from a Disney World vacation in March of 2001, my family started out on our second major crisis. Colton told us there was something strange on his carpet, under the window. When we moved the bed away from the wall we discovered large patches of yellow, green and black mold growing on the carpet, on the walls and up the bedpost.

As toxic mold was the current scourge in the insurance industry, my first call went to an industrial hygienist. From all of the material I had been reading in the trade publications, I was aware of the potential health hazards. Two days later, we got the dreaded news. There were three strains of toxic mold growing in the samples. The spores had become airborne, and the particulates in the air had become 10,000 times higher than acceptable levels. We were instructed to leave our home immediately, with nothing but the clothes on our backs.

One phone call and our world had been turned upside-down. What a shock! I will never forget coming home from work to give Kristi the bad news. What a strange event! We couldn't even begin to comprehend the magnitude of our loss.

Next, we had to pick up our 6-year-old boys from school and explain this bizarre situation to them. We ended up spending two weeks in a hotel and another five months in a rented house with rented furniture that smelled like smoke. The boys lost nearly everything they owned. Colton had many health problems which now made sense. And Dylan became anxious for the first time in his young life.

After additional testing, the experts determined that the contamination had affected our entire home. An inspection of the construction indicated that the roof had been installed incorrectly and had for years allowed rainwater to enter the walls. The combination of moisture and a warm, dark, confined space produced an ideal breeding ground. Eventually, the mold grew through the walls and onto the interior surfaces. As the mold dried, it infiltrated the air.

The reason we were told not to remove anything from the home was that everything in the house had been contaminated. The microscopic mold spores had settled on all of the surfaces inside the home. Hard-surfaced items such as tables, desk and dressers could be decontaminated and salvaged. Porous items such as mattresses, couches and carpets had to be removed and immediately destroyed by burning in a safe, controlled environment. Luckily, most of our clothing could be salvaged if cleaned through two cycles at a commercial cleaner.

Early in the ordeal, Kristi broke down and told me she couldn't handle the stress any longer. It had been seven years since our accident, and we were just starting to feel as though we were getting our feet back on the ground. The thought of dealing with another tragedy was too much for her. I told her I would handle the situation and would try my best to keep her out of it. After all, she had been the one to steer us through our last tragedy nearly single-handedly. Now it was my turn.

In many respects, the first phases of the ordeal were the toughest for me. I had to enter the home alone to gather up all of the clothing and linens for commercial laundering. There was no way I was going to let Kristi or the boys go back into that unhealthy environment. By doing so, Kristi would often develop a migraine headache, setting us back for several days.

By this time, it was the middle of June and the summer heat was with us in full measure, making the job all the harder because we had to keep the air conditioning turned off in the house to prevent further circulation of the contaminated air. Protected with only a cloth breathing mask, I would enter the home to retrieve as much as I could. The heat, along with the humid stench of the mold was almost nauseating.

I had to use my white cane to get around, even though I had completely memorized the layout of the house. The environmental contractors had already done significant demolition by this time, and the place was a real war zone. There were damaged building materials lying everywhere, and huge sections of the upstairs flooring had been removed. One missed step and I would come tumbling to the first floor. It was, quite simply, a disaster.

Strange as it may seem, in some ways the challenge invigorated me. After the accident, I was focused on my blindness and my own fragile mental state. I wasn't much help in any decision making process. Now, however, I was back on my game and eager to get down to work. By this point, I felt mentally sharp. After all, I had been running my own business for several years.

As I began steering us through this maze of insurance contracts, adjusters, and the entire claims process, my experience in the insurance field helped enormously. Even though we were in the midst of a complicated project, I continued to gain confidence in my abilities. But the process became extremely confusing and complicated because of the conflicting information and recommendations I received from just about everyone involved. The most notable contradictions came from the industrial hygienists. One of them told me emphatically that breathing air contaminated with toxic mold spores could cause cancer, lung disease or mental disorders. Conversely, another hygienist told me the mold was harmless and that I could eat it with no side effects!

During inspections of our home, hygienist #1 would put on a bio-hazard suit, complete with a hood and breathing apparatus. Hygienist #2 would enter the house with absolutely no protection. Hygienist #1 referred to #2 as a "member of the flat earth society." Hygienist #2 thought #1 was a reactionary. Just to keep it interesting, a third hygienist was brought in for testing. (Who, by the way got very sick with a 'mysterious illness' just after he inspected our home). He was down somewhere between the extremes of #1 and #2.

I based my conclusions, finally, on the health effects that the mold seemed to have had on my family and me. Before we evacuated our home, we had suffered from a number of mysterious ailments. Kristi was in a state of constant fatigue, also suffering regular migraine headaches and a suppressed immune system. Colton had developed a respiratory problem and required nightly breathing treatments. Except for chicken, rice, soy and some fruits, he was allergic to just about every food. As for me, I was suffering from fatigue. I did fine during the week, when I spent most of the day away from home. On the weekends, however, I felt drugged and simply wanted to sleep. Within less than three months after we moved out, virtually all of our physical symptoms had disappeared. Kristi described it as "coming out of a fog." Colton's allergies subsided and he no longer required an inhaler.

Unfortunately, the industrial hygienists weren't the only ones who were giving us conflicting advice. The environmental contractors' recommendations varied greatly on how the house should be remediated. One contractor simply wanted to encase the damaged wall studs in foam and replace the drywall. The other wanted to completely remove and replace any areas where the mold was growing. There was an enormous difference in cost and time between these two methods. To complicate matters even further, industrial hygienist #1 wanted to tear the house down and start from scratch. But with the help of my attorneys, Patrick McGroder and Shannon Clark, I was able to make informed decisions, and we eventually got the house remediated.

In all, it took almost two years to complete the renovation of our home. Those two years were a real nightmare for us. It seemed there was a never-ending series of problems attacking us from all sides. Between the environmental consultants, remediation specialists, remodeling contractors, insurance adjusters and lawyers, it seemed that everyone was heaping stress upon us. It was probably the most complex, frustrating and at times demoralizing process we have ever endured.

After remediation, it was time to rebuild the house. Thankfully, we got lucky and selected a quality contractor, Logos Builders. The construction went well and it wasn't long before they had our home looking like brand new. As an added bonus, I became friends with the owner of Logos, John Cavness, who is now a spiritual mentor for me.

In 2003, we finally moved back in. We were grateful to have our home once again, something we've learned not to take for granted.

Chapter 26

Death of a Close Friend

On October 31, 2001, I got one of those earth shattering calls—the ones where you immediately know that something has gone terribly wrong. I was at my office when my friend Dino Paul called to see if Bob Schaefer, one of my closest friends, was OK.

What a strange question, I thought. Dino and Bob didn't really know each other all that well, and it seemed strange that he would be calling about anything having to do with Bob.

Dino had heard that Bob Schaefer died of a heart attack that morning. At first, I thought he must have gotten Bob confused with his father Bill. Bob was only 36 years old and, while not in the greatest health, he was much too young for a heart attack. I also reasoned that I surely would have heard about such an event before Dino.

My first call was to Bob's office. I got his voice mail. A follow-up call to his cell phone provided the same result. Not unusual, I thought, as he wasn't the hardest working guy in the business. That being said, a sick feeling began to well up in the pit of my stomach.

Not wanting to bother his wife, Courtney, I called Dave Robertson, Bob's best friend. I asked Dave, as calmly as I could, if he knew where he was. The long pause told me everything I needed to know.

"Bob's gone," was all Dave could get out.

Taken so early from us, one of my best friends and supporters, gone in an instant, leaving behind a grieving wife and two young children, William and our goddaughter, Hannah. How quickly the tides of life turn. Courtney, who only a few years earlier had been there with Bob to help Kristi and me through our tragedy, was now in need of our help.

Thank goodness, Kristi was there for all of us once again. I was really hit hard by Bob's death and wasn't much good at consoling Courtney.

Kristi remained very strong through the whole ordeal, something I can't say for myself. I fought back tears every time I spoke with her or the kids.

Courtney called me at work a couple of days after Bob's death to tell me she had donated his eyes to a cornea bank. The impact of the gesture that Bob would be providing sight to someone in his death was overwhelming to me. I dropped to the floor in my office and cried for a good half an hour.

At the funeral, I told the following story:

"A few years ago, Bob and I went fishing in the Arizona White Mountains in a little canoe. For those of you who have never been in a canoe, it really is a balancing act to keep upright. Can you imagine a big guy and a blind man trying to stay afloat in a tipsy canoe? The trip was made more exciting by all of the rocking back and forth as we cast our lines and pulled in each catch. That trip truly represented to me what it meant to be friends with Bob: kind of exciting, kind of an adventure, and always a wild ride."

As Murphy's Law would have it, the 9th Annual Welker Invitational Golf tournament was scheduled to played just two days after Bob's death. We dedicated the tournament to him. It was a very difficult day but provided us all with some time to grieve together.

In the months after Bob's death, his children, William and Hannah, spent a lot of time at our house. Courtney needed the down time to recover, and the Schaefer kids get along well with Colton and Dylan.

Whenever William and Colton spend time together, it brings a smile to my face. They sound like Bob and I would have if we had been friends at that age. William often tells Colton some greatly exaggerated story and Colton buys it, hook, line and sinker, just like I did with Bob. Sometimes William says something that sounds like his Dad, and it brings a lump to my throat.

I couldn't imagine the pain these children were enduring at the loss of their Dad. On one occasion, as I was lecturing William about the importance of treating his Mom with more respect, I explained to him that she had just lost her husband and needed to be treated accordingly.

"What about me?" William replied through his tears. "I lost my Dad!"

Ouch! So ended my brief grief-counseling career.

In time, Courtney remarried. She found a great guy, Dale Gorder, and she has put her life back together. Dale has some huge shoes (or should I say flip-flops) to fill, but I think he is up to the task. The kids are doing well and the older William gets, the more he sounds like his Dad.

Bob's stay on this planet was short, but his life impacted a lot of people. I miss him very much, but know that he now resides in the mansion God prepared for him. His death was another reminder of how temporal our stay on this earth is. All of our days are numbered, and it is up to us to make the most of them.

Part Five:

"My cup runneth over."

Chapter 27

Snow Skiing

One of my favorite activities before the accident was snow skiing. I was introduced to the sport when I was 18 and I was immediately hooked. Contrary to popular belief, by the way, Arizona has a couple of nice ski areas. However, I did most of my skiing in the rocky mountains of Colorado and Utah.

In college, I spent my spring breaks skiing in Telluride, Colorado, Lake Tahoe, Nevada and Park City, Utah. I not only enjoyed the sport, but I really enjoyed the social life that went with it. I could probably write a whole book on skiing and après-ski alone.

After the accident, though, I resigned myself to the fact that this part of my life was over. Without giving it much thought, I figured that it would be impossible for a blind person to ski. How wrong I was!

My good friend Dino Paul owns and operates a graphic design business called "Dino Design" (pretty creative, huh?) Before my accident, he had done some graphic design work for the United States Blind Athletes Association (was that irony or fate?). In the course of that work he had interviewed an individual named Michael May, an accomplished blind downhill skier who had won several gold medals at the Para-Olympics for disabled athletes. He also held the downhill speed skiing record for blind skiers—an extended run at over 70 miles per hour. This was more than impressive to me; it was unbelievable! I had never skied anywhere near this speed when I could see!

Michael had been blinded in a chemical explosion when he was very young. The fact that he was able to achieve so much as a blind person really lifted my spirits. Beyond his skiing prowess, he was accomplished at many other sports, and he was also a successful businessman, husband and father.

With Dino's help, I was able to contact Michael during the fall of 1994. The first time we talked, Michael apologized for the delay in getting back to me. He'd been out wind surfing and got back later than he had anticipated. My first question was, obviously, how does a blind guy wind surf? After several conversations with Michael and after listening to his audiotapes, I figured that some day—well into the future—I might give snow skiing as a blind person a try. I certainly had no intention of trying it anytime soon. Nonetheless, Michael May served as an important role model for me.

As luck (or misfortune) would have it, Dave Littman, my friend Courtney Schaefer's step-brother, was a ski instructor for the disabled. When he heard our story, he offered to provide me with lessons. After I talked with him and decided to try, Dave suggested I bring one of my friends along so he could teach him to be my guide. So before I could come up with any good reasons to delay this terrifying plan, I asked Dino, and he quickly volunteered. If only he had known what a major commitment he was in for! On the other hand, he probably thought it through and decided it was his destiny.

In case you have not figured it out by now, I am not the bravest, most courageous person God has ever put on the planet. While not a complete 'chicken', I would certainly never classify myself as a risk-taker (even though I have a sweatshirt with the logo "No Fear" printed on it, Dino has suggested that I produce a new line called "All Fear").

Nevertheless, in March of 1995, Dino and I packed up our ski gear and headed to Lake Tahoe to meet Dave at the North Star ski resort. I had skied at this resort when I could see, and I remembered it as a fairly easy mountain. Something told me I would not think the same thing this time around.

We stayed at the Calneva Hotel & Casino, a landmark of sorts on the North shore, a resort that Frank Sinatra had once owned. Before hitting the slopes, we decided to try our luck at the craps tables.

After we explained to the pit boss that I was blind and Dino would be managing my chips for me, he let us play uninterrupted. While I'm not the greatest craps player in the world, I did think I was having a fairly successful run at the table that night.

Later, while cashing out my chips, I commented to Dino that I thought I had done a little better. He responded in a matter of fact tone that I probably would have if he hadn't run out of chips and started stealing mine half way through. Later, as I lay in bed that night, I remember thinking: "Am I sure I want to put my life and my limbs into this guy's hands?"

The next morning, less than one year after my accident, I found myself standing at the top of the slopes, preparing to ski again.

To be honest, I don't remember being very nervous that first day. I think I was too oblivious to the danger that lay in store. As they say, ignorance is bliss.

For the first run down the hill, instructor Dave told me to hold onto the back-end of two bamboo poles, one in each hand. He then skied in front of me, holding the front of the poles. I found this method too restrictive. I was uncomfortable skiing without my own poles, and my balance didn't seem to be as sure.

For the next run, Dave suggested that we abandon the bamboo poles; he would simply ski in front of me, calling out the turns. Using this method, I lost the comfort of being physically attached to my guide but was also left with the freedom of skiing on my own—and I liked it!

After getting used to listening to a guide telling me when to turn, I got into a rhythm and began to re-experience the feeling of skiing down a hill. It was very frightening, seeing nothing but black where the ski trail used to be, filled with skiers I couldn't see, unpredictable bumps, changing grades—and all those trees bordering the trail! On the other hand, I was skiing! It was a 'green' run—for beginners—but it was the scariest run I had ever made. I felt the hard packed snow running under my skis. I felt the wind on my face and heard the sounds of other skiers. As I planted my poles and made my turns, I suddenly realized that I was enjoying myself. Terrified, but exhilarated!

During the chairlift ride, I was feeling pretty proud of myself. I felt that I could actually do this; I could ski as a blind person.

At the top of the hill, Dave asked Dino if he thought he was ready to guide me down the next run. My confidence suddenly evaporated. Was

Dino ready to guide his blind friend, who only had a grand total of two runs under his belt?

Now, don't get me wrong, Dino's a great friend and I trust him, but this is the same guy that spent a summer driving an old school bus around the country with one of his friends riding on the roof.

In typical Dino fashion, he calmly said he was ready. He sounded so sure of himself that I figured he really was. So after some brief instruction, off we went.

Next thing I knew, I was skiing along to Dino's clear and concise commands. My long-time friend sounded as though he had been a ski guide for the blind his whole life. I think he knew this day had been coming for quite a while, and I think he *knew* he was ready.

I've been on many ski trips since that first outing, and it is rare that I'm comfortable with anyone else as my ski guide. To date, Dino and I have done ten seasons together and most often function like a well-oiled machine.

The sport, for us, has changed from an individual one to a team concept. For a successful run, we are reliant on each other. If one of us is off or makes a mistake, the results might be disastrous. One missed turn, one miscue, and I might end up running into a tree or off a cliff. While these events rarely occur, miscues have left me flailing, falling or stopping in panic more than a time or two.

I should note here that the vast majority of the on-slope mistakes are mine. My accuracy rate on the "right" and "left" commands is probably 98%. It's that 2% error ratio which has sometimes proven hazardous.

Dino says that skiing with me is worse than skiing with a girl. (Don't get mad at me! Dino's the one who said it). Remember, he's from the "so you're blind, let's move on" crowd. We do, however, have our shining moments on the slopes. When we're skiing, it's all business. If I am dogging it, he'll let me know, and if I get sloppy with my form, he will correct me. I certainly wouldn't have achieved the level of success I have with anyone else as my guide.

Over the years, several of our buddies have joined the trips. These occasions have turned into great vacations and a chance to spend time with old friends. On one trip, we trained our friend Chris Hahn to be my guide. While I survived the event, he turned out to be a lousy guide. The problem was that Chris is too nice a guy to be an effective guide. He was continually apologizing for this or that. If I turned too short or too long he would take full responsibility for the next several seconds. While he was telling me how terribly sorry he was that he failed to mention that last drop off, he would forget to tell me about the next turn I needed to make. It certainly was an exciting trip down the mountain!

I have had some other guides over the years, but Dino is the person I am most comfortable with. As long as his understanding wife, Jenny, will let me keep borrowing him, I planto teke full advantage.

One of the most exciting moments on the slopes with Dino came the day we skied the slalom NASTAR racecourse. I started at the top of the course at the gates, with Dino a few feet below. As the starting tone rang, I came out of the gate and Dino was at my side. He guided me through the gates as he skied next to them. It was a real charge, racing around the gates against the clock. A buddy of ours, Brian Scott, raced that day, too. I tell everyone that I beat him. I don't know if that's completely accurate, but it makes for a better story.

One of Dino's many strengths is that he has some great ways of motivating me. He can usually talk me into making one more run or getting back on the skis after a bad crash. One day, I didn't feel like skiing and I was trying to find excuses to get out of it. "All these people up here want to see a blind guy ski," he said. "They don't want to see a blind guy sitting in the lodge drinking coffee."

"Good point," I thought. He got me on the slopes that day.

Over the years, we have perfected the blind guide process. For precise communication, we now use two-way radios with headset connections. I can tell by the inflection and duration of Dino's tone the degree and sharpness of the turn he wants me to make. He skis 20 to 50 feet behind me and keeps me posted with pertinent information such as slope steepness, snow conditions, obstructions and wayward skiers.

I wear a bib that identifies me as a blind skier, and Dino wears one that reads "guide." The bibs are a safety precaution; they help us stand out on the slopes. Unfortunately, some of the other skiers on the hill don't seem to see our large, orange bibs.

On the slopes, skiers sometimes engage in interesting conversations. For example, one afternoon, with both of us tiring a bit, we stopped for a breather on opposite sides of an intermediate run. A skier we passed earlier stopped beside Dino and asked, pointing to me, "That guy's not really blind, is he?" Dino has little tolerance for people like that. I, on the other hand, took it as a compliment that the man thought I could see.

On another afternoon, I was relaxing at the lodge and Dino was skiing by himself. He was still wearing his "Guide" bib and a lady sharing a lift chair with him asked, "Are you the guide for the blind skier I saw earlier?"

Dino began nervously looking around into the passing trees and responded, with a straight face, "Yes, have you seen him anywhere? I'd really like to find him before it gets too dark." He says that the lady believed him and that I should have seen her expression! Of course, he finally explained what was really going on and that I wasn't smashed up against some tree somewhere.

On another recent trip, Dino and I skied past a member of the Ski Patrol. They were bringing someone down the hill in a sled, the method typically used to get injured skiers to the bottom of the mountain. Later, in the lodge, a lady stopped Dino and asked if he was the guy who was guiding the blind skier. She went on to tell Dino that she had been the person in the sled. Apparently, she had become scared on the slopes and the Ski Patrol had to bring her down.

"I just can't believe that blind guy could ski down the mountain so well," she told Dino. "I guess I just need to be blind so I can't see how scary the runs are."

"I wouldn't recommend that option," was Dino's dry response.

While skiing at Park City, Utah, Dino and I came close to having our team skiing concept hauled into court. We were navigating an intermediate run, minding our own business, when a lady suddenly veered left and skied directly in front of me. As I was skiing straight down the hill, I was fortunate to miss her, skiing only over the backs of her skis, and I wasn't even aware of what really happened. It all went down in a matter of two seconds, nowhere near enough time for Dino to warn me. I must interject here that those inconsiderate skiers who suddenly change direction on a run without checking for uphill traffic drive Dino and me crazy. It's bad enough when it happens to a sighted skier, but when someone cuts in front of a blind skier, reaction time is delayed, of course, and corrections are difficult to make.

Oftentimes, too, Dino and I are skiing at a quicker pace than most of the other skiers on the hill, which increases the likelihood of such an incident. For this reason, Dino must not only be watching me, but he also has to be aware of everyone within 50 to 100 feet of me. Usually, Dino just yells at the clueless skier. With his commanding Italian voice and cool demeanor, he succinctly explains the transgression to the offender as he passes by them. After they figure out they have cut off a blind skier, I can usually hear them apologizing all the way down the hill.

After this particular incident, however, I didn't hear Dino's usual chastisement of the skiing infraction. Instead, Dino commanded me to stop. Then, on my headphones, I heard Dino's voice asking if she was OK. After he spoke several minutes with her, Dino told me that I had skied behind her and she had fallen down.

I was worried and sidestepped 50 feet up the slope to check on her. After we were assured she was fine, Dino and I were on our way. At the time, she seemed a bit embarrassed about the whole scenario.

I didn't give it another thought until a couple of days later, when the resort office phoned me at my hotel room. The resort manager wanted to get statements regarding the incident. Apparently, the day after the incident, she came to their office with her knee wrapped in a support brace, walking on crutches. She was professing that the resort should never allow blind skiers on the hill because it was too dangerous.

The National Ability Center, located in Park City, is known nationwide for its role in training disabled people to ski. Their students include not only blind people, but paraplegics, quadriplegics and the mentally disabled. This tremendous organization advocates for these individuals and supports their ability to enjoy mountain skiing. The lady I skied too close to didn't agree with this concept, apparently feeling that disabled people should just stay at home. By doing that, according to her reasoning, they wouldn't hurt any of the "normal" people.

She actually did file a legal action, and the process dragged on for several months until, one day, I got a call from her attorney. He had already spoken with Dino and wanted to get my side of the story. After I relayed my version of the event to him, he asked what I thought was a rather strange question.

"You know," he started, "I ski in Park City sometimes. The next time I'm there, do you want to make a couple of runs together?"

"Wouldn't that be a conflict of interest?" I asked.

"No, not at all," he responded. "I am dropping this client as of today, and I think it would be fun to ski with you."

That was the last we ever heard about the complaint. Dino wanted to sue her for cutting me off, but I talked him out of it.

These days we usually ski at Deer Valley, Utah, which is a great mountain for blind skiers. The runs are well groomed, and they are fairly consistent with minimal bumps. This resort limits the number of skiers on the slopes and they don't allow snow boarders, both of which are unneeded distractions for a blind skier. They also have the best food of any ski resort I have ever been to.

We have learned over the years that skiing steeper runs with more pitch provides the best skiing conditions. These runs allow me to get into a rhythm of planting and turning. The times I enjoy most are when I am thinking of nothing but skiing. For those few minutes, I don't feel disabled. Instead, I feel like I did before I lost my sight. It gives me a great sense of freedom to be skiing so fast.

On easier, flatter runs, I start thinking too much and have less fun. Cat walks and transition areas are more nerve wracking than rush hour traffic. Lift lines are also a hassle. We have discovered that Dino gives me more directions in the lift line than on the trails. But don't worry, fellow skiers, I don't require the lift chairs to be slowed to get on them.

January of 2006 may have been the high water mark of my skiing career. For the first time, I got to ski with my sons. We put them in ski school and we were worried that they may not get the hang of it. We should have known better. They were skiing all over the hill and I had trouble keeping up with them.

The interesting thing was that I'm not sure who was prouder of whom. Of course, I was the proud father as I listened to my boys swooshing down the hill. But they, on the other hand, were excitedly urging me on as they skied along side me. All in all, a good time was had by both father and sons. It was a very special moment I don't think I will ever forget.

Until recently, I thought the entire concept of a blind guy skiing was a notable achievement and was pretty proud of my accomplishment. But that was before I read a book by Eric Weihenmayer, a blind mountain climber, entitled *Touch the Top of the World*. In the book, he describes how he has successfully climbed several mountains, including Mount McKinley and Mount Everest. While listening to the trials of him sleeping in a bag nailed to the side of a rock face or climbing along a three-foot-wide ice bridge over a 12,000 foot drop-off, my skiing along a well groomed trail doesn't sound all that dangerous. My idea of roughing it is a day lodge without gourmet coffee.

I spoke with Eric once, and he tried to talk me into rock climbing. I explained it was something I didn't do as a sighted person and certainly didn't plan to attempt as a blind guy. In retrospect, this is probably why Eric is able to climb those dangerous mountains. He can't see how terrifying those drop offs are. I, on the other hand, have watched documentaries of those places and fully understand that man simply wasn't meant to go there.

Chapter 28

Other Recreational Activities and Hobbies

Blindness has changed the way I do almost everything in my life, including recreational activities and hobbies. After acclimating to blindness, I soon learned that my entertainment options were virtually limitless.

I still enjoy watching movies and TV (yes, blind people do these things). For a while after the accident, I thought there would be no reason to watch a movie or TV. Since I couldn't see, I rationalized, I couldn't follow the action, so a movie or TV show wouldn't be entertaining. Boy, was I wrong!

The first movie I can remember 'watching' as a blind person was "A Few Good Men," with Tom Cruise and Jack Nicholson. It was broadcast on a movie channel at home, and I found I actually enjoyed 'watching' it. It helped, of course, that I had seen the movie before I lost my sight. I decided to give it another try.

One afternoon, Kristi and I ventured out to the movie theater to see "Forrest Gump." At first, I just felt stupid sitting there, not being able to see anything. Then I began crying because I was feeling so sorry for myself. Before long, though, I started to get interested in the story.

As luck would have it, this was a great movie for a blind person. Forrest Gump (Tom Hanks) narrated the entire movie. This allowed me to follow the story line and use my newly discovered "theater of the mind."

The first movie we went to with Colton and Dylan in tow was "Toy Story." Because I then knew what to expect, I wasn't so emotional. As I sat in the theater with a son sitting on each leg, I decided there was more to going to the movies than seeing the screen. Holding onto my boys as they laughed and giggled made the entire experience worth it.

When the boys were younger, I spent hours on the couch watching videos with them. Like many parents, it was a big part of our 'together time'. Our collection included many of the usual animated ones including Disney, Warner Brothers and super hero movies. I have no idea how many times I watched 'Aladdin.' I can still quote lines from that movie!

The first live action video Dylan liked when he was about three was a Lassie movie. He is a real animal lover so it was no surprise. At 5 o'clock one morning, he came in and began tapping the video against my head while quietly whispering, "Assie, Assie, Daddy!"

He was so cute; I actually got up and put it in for him.

Another one of our favorite shows was "The Andy Griffith Show." We have several video episodes, and many of Barney Fife's lines have become standard sayings in our home. The staying power of this classic TV show is amazing. It helps that I have seen every episode (at least five times!) and I can visualize the characters. This is true of all of my old favorites like "Seinfeld," "Star Trek," "Green Acres" and the "Star Wars" movies (the first three episodes), "Top Gun," "The Jerk," and just about any other Steve Martin movie.

A unique phenomenon of my blindness is that I often believe I have seen things that I haven't. This applies to people, movies, TV shows, cars—just about anything. (This drives Kristi crazy.)

For years, I was under the incorrect assumption that I had seen the NBC-TV show "Friends." Kristi and I 'watched' the show frequently and I was sure that I had seen the early episodes. I thought the first show had aired just before the accident.

I was absolutely convinced that I knew what the set looked like, what Ross looked like, and clearly remembered his monkey. Kristi and I had several discussions on the topic. Even when I was unable to correctly identify Ross' physical characteristics (hair color, facial appearance, etc.), I still thought I had seen the show. I figured that he had just changed his looks over the years. As for the women on the show, I told Kristi that they pretty much all looked alike.

Then came September of 2003 and the show's 10th anniversary season. The promos proclaimed that the show's first season was the fall of 1994, five months after our accident. I told Kristi that I must have seen an early test episode. They do that sometimes, don't they? I finally had to admit to myself that I had never actually seen the show.

Another interesting thing happens when I listen to an audio book and then 'see' the movie. Normally, when this situation happens I visualize all of the characters, locations and scenes and create the story in my mind's eye when I listen to the book.

Then, when I 'see' the movie, I visualize the exact same things. The characters, the scenes and the landscaping are just as I pictured them when I read the book.

I became aware of this recently while watching Stephen King's movie, "Dream Catcher," a book I had read only a couple of months before. I suddenly realized that everything was the same. The aliens, Jonesy, Mr. Grey, the Hole-in-the-Wall cabin, all were just as I had imagined them. Oftentimes I think I 'see' a better movie than sighted people. I am no longer visually disappointed at a movie's adaptation of the book—at least not in terms of the characters, the settings, the landscaping and so forth.

These days, we regularly watch TV, and we are frequent moviegoers, both as a couple and as a family. I would honestly have to say that I enjoy going to the movies more now than I did when I could see. The AMC chain offers a wonderful service for the blind called "Descriptive Video." This is a service which describes the on-screen action of a movie through headphones in between the normal dialogue. It really enhances the movie-going experience. It also helps Kristi enjoy the movie because she doesn't have to keep me apprised of critical visual plot elements.

Some genres, such as action, adventure and science fiction, just don't work well without the visual description. Others, like comedies, biographies and movies with a lot of dialogue are better suited for blind audiences.

We recently took the boys to see the latest release of "King Kong." This was a great example of how the visual describer makes movies more enjoyable for the blind. Since it has long action sequences with no dialogue and is three-and-a-half hours long, I would have fallen asleep before I finished my popcorn if not for the visual describer.

ଛ

During the years of my misspent youth, I was in a bad rock band. I don't mean" bad" in the current vernacular which means "cool", but "bad" in that we weren't very good. Our main claim to fame was that we were loud—very loud.

Loud was important because of the type of music we were playing; namely, hard rock like Grand Funk Railroad, Kiss, Deep Purple and the Rolling Stones. These were heady times for us and we were riding the wave. In addition to playing at school dances, we played at parties and just about anywhere else that would have us. The fact that we rarely did repeat performances was, I think, more attributable to the fact that we didn't play any slow songs. We didn't like them because they were . . . well, slow.

We formed the band in Chris Hahn's bedroom with his brother, Corey who played the drums. I played guitar and I taught Chris how to play bass guitar. Of minor concern was that I did not know how to play bass myself and wasn't very good on guitar to begin with.

"How much different could it be from playing a regular guitar?" I reasoned. We proceeded on that incorrect assumption for the length of the band's dubious history.

We called the band "Burn." Those early days were very exciting, and we were pretty sure we were going to be famous. We lasted several weeks using Chris's bedroom as a practice studio before we ran into a problem that would plague us during our entire rock and roll career.

At that time, we had only three songs in our repertoire ("Tobacco Road," "Gloria" and "Smoke on the Water"), but we played very long versions to compensate for our short play list. We were about 30 minutes into "Tobacco Road," when I heard this incredible pounding on the door. Then, the door flew open and there stood Al Hahn, Chris and Corey's Dad, who is generally a gentle man. He was literally as tall as the door frame.

He told us in no uncertain terms that if we played one more note of that song, our instruments would be crushed.

This major incident started our house-to-house migration from one band member's abode to another's. With our success came more members and more equipment. Soon, we would take over entire living rooms with our amplifiers, drums and keyboards. We would usually last a couple of months at each location before we were asked to leave by the parents, the neighbors, the police or all three.

To compensate for our less than gifted musical abilities, we needed more than just volume. To fill this void, we opted for special effects. On stage, we used rockets, flares, dry ice for the illusion of smoke, and we had a light show that was quite elaborate for a garage band. For special gigs, we would don face paint (a la Kiss).

The split-up of "Burn" was not the horrible ordeal often associated with bands. It was the crossing of two inevitable realities: 1) we lacked the talent and/or motivation to make a career out of rock and roll and 2) we had to finish college.

In the post-band days and years, I didn't play the guitar much. Unfortunately, I was too busy with my education, my career, and the rest of life's experiences to keep up with this hobby. I guess I may have been "burned" out on the whole guitar playing experience.

For the first year or two after losing my sight, I didn't give much thought to playing the guitar again. I still had too many other issues on my plate, mainly, putting my life back together as a blind man, working on my career, and being a new Dad.

As I started to put things back together, I asked Kristi to take me down to the music store so I could buy an acoustic guitar. I was desperately searching for things I could still do.

Up to this point, I had played an electric guitar because in our band, we played rock and roll. Much of this style required the use of frets far up the neck of the guitar and demanded lots of precise and swift horizontal hand movements. I decided that my blindness was going to prevent me from successfully accomplishing these placements. With an acoustic guitar, however, I could still play open chords, which don't require big movements up the neck. With some practice, I have been able to improve this style of playing to a level I never achieved on the electrified instrument. If I really concentrate, I can also play some bar chords. Well, with this entire guitar playing success, I just had to go out and buy myself a Fender Telecaster guitar and Peavey amplifier. I am back to where I was 30 years ago; electrified, loud, and still not very good.

My guitar hobby has changed dramatically and, whenever time allows, I enjoy playing very much. My taste in music has changed to softer rock, ballads and contemporary Christian music.

My method for figuring out songs and storing them has changed considerably, too. I can't just go to the music store and buy sheet music, so I had to come up with an alternate method. Now, I figure out the chords and lyrics to a given song and create a document in my word processor. Whenever I want to play that song, I will pull up that file; refresh my memory by listening to the document, and play away. For the lyrics I forget, no problem. I just make them up, like everyone else.

Some of my most enjoyable musical times these days are when my family gets together for "band night." Kristi and my sisters Cheryl and Janice sing, and Neth Sullivan—Cheryl's partner—and I play guitars. Joe Sauer, Janice's husband, sometimes joins us to sing a couple of songs. We go on for hours and sometimes we sound pretty good. Well, we think so, anyway.

The first night we got together, I was nervous. I hadn't played guitar in front of anyone since before the accident, and wasn't sure I could pull it off. Neth is a real guitar player, and I was worried the whole thing would end up being an embarrassing waste of time. I was worried that my inability to watch his hands for chord progressions and visual cues would foul me up and cause musical chaos. As it turned out, my worrying was the only thing that was a waste of time. Neth couldn't have been more accommodating. He was very patient and helpful with chord progressions and teaching me riffs I didn't know. Using a trial and error method, we figured out a way to put the songs together. Before long, we were knocking them out one after another. Kristi and my sisters, of course, made the occasion very comfortable. Eventually, I was taking control of the session, just like the old days. (Man, how do these people live with me?).

One thing I enjoy most about our band nights is, I don't feel disabled while I am playing the guitar and singing. I am "flying!" For those few minutes, I am neither better nor worse off than anyone else in the room. For that short period of time, I am not disabled (except for my lack of singing skills, that is).

ଧ

In November of 2002, I started a new hobby, an HO scale-model train layout. I had wanted to do this since I was a kid. And now, with twin eight-year-old sons, I had the perfect excuse. I figured it was a very tactile project and decided to give it a try.

I recruited Neth Sullivan, my guitar-playing partner, to take me to Home Depot for the project supplies. The basic items included a 4'x8' sheet of plywood, a similar sized sheet of Styrofoam, edging and paint.

The first phases of the project involved having the boys help me paint the edging I had cut to fit the plywood. I decided early on that painting was a task better left to them. From there, I glued on the Styrofoam sheet, the fake grass and attached the molding. I now had a huge piece of plywood that looked like a putting green.

It was time to bring my large, budding project from the garage into the house. By the way, Kristi offered absolutely no resistance. Do I have a great wife or what?

My success in this early stage gave me the confidence to believe that I could not only do this project, but that it would be fun.

I have spent more time on this project than I will ever admit to, and I am embarrassingly proud of it. The boys, as well as many neighbor kids, have pitched in from time to time. But I have done the vast majority of the planning and construction myself.

My train scene is a rural area with a recreational lake and an industrial area. The buildings include Lenny's Clam Box restaurant, Bud's Convenience Store, a train station, a church, the Hoffa Cement Factory, a sand and gravel operation, Bill's Garage, Ted's Hot Dogs, a haunted house, and a ranch with a barn. Intertwined in the setting are over 45 feet of train track, two tunnels, and a lake with boats. My display includes people shopping, hiking, swimming, traveling and working. The lake has an island in it, and for this reason, I have three passenger cars named "Rock Island."

I am a regular at Roy's Train World, the local model railroad store. Between Roy's and the Internet, I have spent more hours and money than I care to admit. I wouldn't be able to venture a guess, actually, at how many hours I have invested in the railroad project. Because I have built every section of the layout, I am very familiar with each and every detail. While I am working on it, I am obviously doing so "in the dark." When I am away from the project, oddly enough, I have a very clear vision of what the model looks like. Every building, mountain or train comes into clear focus. At times, I have even dreamed about the model as if I have seen it (I know, I know. It's probably starting to sound like I am a little bit obsessed about all of this but I'm not!).

While just a hobby, I think it serves as a small example of the abilities of people who are blind. Over time, I have discovered that most people have no idea what the blind are capable of accomplishing. In my own unique way, I am here to show the world that people who are blind can do almost anything if they put their mind to it.

ß

In February of 2004, at a fundraiser for ACBVI, I played a game called beep ball. It is basically softball for the blind and visually impaired. Specialized equipment includes a softball with a beeper inside and two foam bases with beepers. A sighted pitcher, who is on the batter's team, pitches the ball and the batter tries to hit it. If the ball is hit, one of the bases at first or third starts beeping. The batter then tries to find the base before a fielder finds the ball. Sound confusing? It is.

My first two at bats were frustrating, and I didn't even make contact with the ball. On my third at bat, however, I actually hit the ball. After determining which base was beeping, I quickly took off running to find it.

As luck would have it, I was safe and a run was scored. This insignificant swing of the bat was probably the most exciting base hit I ever had. I left the event with mixed emotions. On the one hand, it was somewhat depressing because I played baseball all through high school, and played softball in my 20s and part of the excitement of playing was seeing the action. It was discouraging to be aware of how much I was missing since the game was now invisible to me. On the other hand, though, it felt good being on the field again. It was awesome to feel the grass under my feet, to anticipate making a play and to swing the bat..

This beep ball event is a great fundraiser, especially for sighted people who come out to play. All it takes to 'level the playing field' is a blindfold. Can you see (pun intended) how that can help sighted folks get a small taste of what it's like to be blind? It gets 'em every time, and it's an accurate rendering, both physically and emotionally, that they can take home with them.

Chapter 29

Tricks of the Blind

Adapting to the world without use of a major sense I had relied on for 37 years has been a major, life-changing undertaking for me. I have had to learn new ways of doing almost everything. Some of these new ways—these "tricks," as I call them—I learned from others, but I've developed most of them on my own.

The two biggest 'tricks' to functioning successfully are *memory* and *organization*. I have to remember practically everything I encounter, and I need to develop and learn by rote a system that organizes and leads me through each activity. From the method I use to sort clothes in the closet to the location of everything in my backpack to the positioning and order of the tools on my workbench, I have to commit every detail to memory. I can no longer just go look for something; I need to have it in its place and remember where that place is.

An example of this is when I move the computer. As I am unplugging all of the cords and cables, I have to remember exactly where each goes so I can correctly put it back together. Simple things like crossing the mouse and keyboard cords, or plugging the printer into the scanner outlet, will prevent the computer from working. It's not a major deal, and I can fix these little mistakes in a matter of minutes most of the time, but there are glitches that can take hours if I don't completely understand, control, identify and remember each operation.

Another example is my work in the garage, tasks like changing inner tubes on the boys' bikes. First, I have to remember where the new tubes are stored. Then it's over to the workbench to find the tools I need for the task. Hopefully, the boys haven't used them and they are exactly where they should be. If the wrench, for instance, has been left on the floor, even if it is right in the middle, I will probably not find it—unless I trip over it.

Then there's the chore of keeping track of the tools while I am working on a project. If I don't keep them in some logical, convenient location, they can get lost. "Lost" for me can be right in front of me, in plain sight.

The job of keeping track of everything often frustrated me. I would get so aggravated when I lost something that I would often give up on the job.

With time, however, has come patience. After over a decade as a blind person, I am better at recognizing the inevitability of this, and I try to be thankful that I can do these tasks at all. It may take me longer to do things, but my frustration level is much lower than it was in the early days. Oh, yes, patience is also a major "trick" for a blind person. I believe, in fact, that it's trick number three. I have become a very patient person.

As a blind person, trying to find something I have dropped on the ground is a major annoyance. It never ceases to amaze me just how far an item can bounce when it's dropped on a hard surface. The "trick" I have learned is to instantly turn on my high-powered ears and listen closely to the item as it bounces, my ears following it until it stops. But if the item is small and doesn't make any noise, like a ball bearing, I just get down on all fours and begin the search.

The favorite 'tricks' I enjoy as a blind person are the ever-growing list of electronic talking gadgets of all sorts. Among the customized items I use are 'talking' personal computers, calculators, dictionaries, watches, pedometers, tape measures, thermostats, thermometers, blood pressure monitors and our telephone's audible caller ID. And that just scratches the surface. There are hundreds more items available through specialized stores and in catalogs.

One of the most frustrating things about being blind is casual conversation, especially the initial exchanges. A lot of people will walk up to me and just start talking, forgetting that I cannot see them, which prevents me from quickly identifying who they are. In these situations, I go into "fake it" mode.

In "fake it" mode, I will pretend to know who they are and hope that I will eventually be able to recognize their voice or pick up some hints along the way. (For example: if they start talking about the boy's school, I figure it must be either a parent or teacher). Also, the setting of the conversation can be helpful. If I am at school, or church, I know that there will be certain people I am more likely to run into. Meeting individuals in unusual places (like running into a client at church), makes it more difficult.

Failing to identify the person I am speaking with can lead to a very awkward encounter. I've had ten-minute conversations with people without a clue as to who they were. It amazes me how many folks I barely know will expect me to recognize them by just their voice.

Experience has taught me that if I ask people who they are, revealing that I didn't recognize their voice, we both feel awkward. I have found it's better to have a conversation with someone I can't identify, than admit I have no idea who they are. This may sound a little strange, but it seems to be the best way of handling the situation. I seem to talk a lot about the weather these days.

Invariably, the people that have the forethought of introducing themselves as soon as they approach me are the same people whose voice I can easily recognize. Chris Hahn is a good example of this. Here is a guy that has been one of my best friends for over thirty years, but he always identifies himself. I think it is because he is so dang polite (Remember, this is the polite guy from the snow skiing chapter).

Don't get me wrong, I don't have a chip on my shoulder about this 'failure to identify' issue. Many times, people will stand back and not approach me at all. Maybe they are uneasy and don't know what to say—but they will not even let me know they are there. For this reason, I'm pleased that so many people feel comfortable enough to approach me.

Another situation that is frustrating (especially for Kristi) is eating at a restaurant. Our first challenge, the hostess, is always trying to hand me a menu. Often, after I tell her that I am blind, she offers to get me a Braille menu. I always decline. It would take me three hours to read the darn thing. By that time, I would have starved to death. Then the second challenge comes when the waitress attempts to take our order. By this time, the hostess has warned the waitress that there is a blind guy in the restaurant and he will require a lot of assistance.

"And what will he have?" the waitress will invariably ask Kristi, referring to me.

"I don't know. Why don't you ask him?" Kristi will answer through a forced, clenched-teeth smile.

Again, I am not complaining. I think that my part-time job is to help educate the general public on the capabilities of the blind—a job, I must add, that I don't mind doing.

Chapter 30

Sad Reminders

On a day-to-day basis, I am pretty comfortable living with my blindness. It occasionally surprises me how 'normal' I feel in spite of my disability. I have discovered ways to overcome the limitations, plan ahead for unforeseen situations, and figure out different ways of doing things.

Sometimes, however, I get sad reminders of some of the things I am missing. It sometimes happens at the most mundane times, or maybe it's at a moment when important, milestone kinds of events are unfolding, —but always when I least expect it. As time goes by, these twinges of regret become less and less frequent. Also, they seem to be a little easier to endure.

One of my earliest sad reminders (the first one that felt like a "breakdown"), happened at Christmas time, nearly eight months after I lost my sight. We were decorating the house, and I was actually enjoying myself. It was mid-morning. I had climbed to our upstairs loft and pulled out some items to take downstairs for decorating our Christmas tree. I picked up a box of decorations, unaware that a glass toy train set was perched atop the box. I made my way to the top of the stairs, turned at the landing where the staircase was, and began walking carefully down the stairs. All at once, the little glass train set slid off the box, tumbling down the stairs, finally crashing onto the tile floor. Instantly, I knew just what had happened! The train set was brand new, and Kristi and I were looking forward to setting it up. The frustration of not being able to see this fragile item that was less than a foot from my face, then having it fall down the stairs and break into a million pieces, was simply too much. I sat down at the foot of the stairs and began to cry. Kristi quickly came to my side to comfort me, but my ineptness at performing this simple task overwhelmed me. "How stupid could I be?" I cried, "If I can't do something as simple as this, what can I do? What good will I *ever* be around here?"

The emotion was uncontrollable. I knew it was self-pity, but in that moment I had absolutely no defense against it. Kristi was wise enough not to minimize it. She let it run its course, and within a few minutes—well, maybe a half-hour—I was able to continue with the day, albeit with a greatly diminished holiday spirit.

Later, upon reflection, I could see that there was a lesson. It was that I would forever have to be extremely careful in every action, every move. Also, I had to recognize that it is OK to go a little slower, be a little more deliberate, and take a little more time. It took me a while to learn this, and today it takes me a little longer to accomplish tasks, but I seldom break things.

All my life I have been a real car buff. When I was young, I was one of those kids who could instantly name the make, model and year of every car on the street. Granted, back then there were not as many makes or models as there are now, but my sure knowledge was impressive indeed, particularly to the adults in my life. And my interest never waned. I maintained my love for cars into adulthood, expanding it into the sport of auto racing.

Many of the cars I have driven over the years would be classics today. At one time or another I owned a showy 1964 Lincoln Continental convertible, a sporty 1964 Fiat 1500, a mint-condition 1976 Pontiac Trans Am, and a Jeep CJ5 with a metallic cherry red fiberglass body. The prize of all of my cars, however, the vehicle I owned at the time of my accident, was my 1973 Porsche 911 Targa. That sleek, fast machine was the four-wheeled love of my life. Soon after I bought it (I am resisting the temptation to call the car "her"), I had it repainted white with flat black trim, added a custom whale tail, and completely rebuilt the engine all by myself. This Porsche wasn't a car I had just picked off a dealer's lot; it had my blood, sweat, and tears in it. I was very proud of this sporty ride and drove it only on weekends and on special occasions. I participated in road rallies and raced it in time trials. If you asked me, I would have to say I was probably a little obsessed.

The World at My Fingertips

After I got home from the hospital, I went through my days without ever giving a single thought to the car—I suppose there were lots of other things to think about, and I didn't have occasion to go to the garage, anyway. But, one day I did wander out there. As I stepped into the cavernous, three-car space, I suddenly thought of the Porsche. I made my way over to the third stall—and there it was! I walked around the familiar vehicle, shaping with my hands and fingers, all of the curves and turns that I knew so well. I clearly pictured the colors of the body, the leather on the seats, the instrument panel—everything. I had spent so much time working and enjoying this car that every detail was permanently etched in my mind.

Awkwardly, I climbed into the driver's seat and put my hands on the steering wheel. At that moment my heart started sinking, and a deep sadness enveloped me. I knew that this would be the last time I would sit in this car and that I would never drive it again. My practical self and my emotional self declared war on each other in that moment, but, my practical self ultimately won out. I realized that in the final analysis, it made no sense to keep a vehicle that I couldn't drive.

Jeff Pawlowski, a friend with some connections in the auto racing industry, told me he could get me onto a nearby test track for one last drive, but I saw no point in that. Without my sight, the excitement of driving the car would be gone, replaced with the fear of damaging the car and perhaps hurting Jeff or myself.

So, I decided to sell the car. I didn't want this painful reminder rusting in my garage. I briefly considered keeping it so I could give it to my sons one day, but I decided that these memories of my old life wouldn't be emotionally healthy.

A few days later, as I stood in the driveway and listened to my Porsche drive off, piloted by its new owner, I knew that a wonderful and exciting chapter of my life had ended and could never be recaptured. The sadness went away after a while, but even today, every time I hear the distinctive sound of a Porsche 911 engine, I think about my four-wheeled love, my 1973 Targa.

ಜ

About a year and a half after the accident, Kristi and I loaded the boys into our van and drove down to visit my folks, who live in the small town of Ajo, Arizona. Ajo is approximately 100 miles southwest of Phoenix, and at that time, that short trip was all we could handle. The boys were still babies, and Kristi and I were still recovering from our injuries, both physically and emotionally.

We arrived in time for the mid-day meal, and after lunch Kristi, Mom and the babies retreated to the house while Dad and I remained seated on the porch. This was the first time I remember Dad and me being alone since the accident. After some awkward small-talk, I made some sort of general comment about my blindness.

"Rock," (his nickname for me), he said, holding back the tears, "you are not going to be blind forever. You are going to get your sight back someday."

"No I'm not, Dad," I said, "I am going to be blind for the rest of my life. I am *permanently* blind."

Well, there it was—permanently! That word brought it all out into the open. Dad and I both began crying as we embraced. My Dad knew full well the medical prognosis. He had been in SICU right after the accident, and he had been with me every step of the way since then. The problem was he hadn't been able to accept it. He seemingly couldn't grasp the fact that his son was going to be forever blind.

Today, I understand a little better his reluctance to accept the obvious. I know that it would be extremely difficult to see your son become disabled, and now that I am a father, I can put myself in his shoes. In all honesty, I can say that I would rather be blind myself than to have one of my sons blinded, and although he's never said it, I'm sure that's how Dad felt.

ಜ

Another tough moment was Halloween of the year that the boys were six. Halloween was a big deal. They loved their costumes even more than the candy. Each year they would revel in putting on costumes and pretending. On the prior two Halloweens they'd been Woody and Buzz Lightyear from "Toy Story," and Aladdin and Jafar.

That year, Colton decided he wanted to be Batman. We ordered him a great costume that featured incredible detail. The mask had little ears on it, and it came with a padded chest vest that simulated muscles. This was especially cute, as Colton was such a thin little guy.

With mom in tow, Dylan and a couple of friends headed down the driveway. I finished tying Colton's cape and quickly checked to make sure that the other costume pieces were correctly in place. By this time, he was very excited so I hurriedly found his candy basket and got him out the door.

As I stood in the doorway, I could hear his little tennis shoes hitting the driveway as he tried to catch up with everyone. I could tell by all of the animated voices that the kids were really excited. I pictured the scene in my mind; a bunch of kids dressed up in their costumes, eager to get Mom moving so they could start collecting their candy.

As I went back inside and shut the door, another of those big blobs of utter sadness descended upon me. In an instant, I was deep into the awful abyss, telling myself how unfair life was. My boy. All dressed up in his Batman costume. And I can't see him! I visualized his little frame, all dressed up like Batman, running down the drive. The more I thought about it, the sadder I became. I leaned against the back of the door. Slowly, bawling like a baby, I slid to the ground and cried from a place so deep inside that it hurt. It occurred to me that this was probably one of those visual moments I would have remembered forever if only I had been able to see it. Instead, all I saw was a sheet of black in front of me. I cried some more. Again, there was a half hour or so of this terrible feeling, then it gradually lifted, and by the time Kristi and the boys returned I had dried up, cleaned up, and decided to put on a happy face for them. They never knew the low place I had plummeted while they were away.

℞

Another such moment took place a couple of years later, when the boys were about eight years old. We were at home watching the movie "Field of Dreams." The boys were really into baseball, so I thought they would enjoy it.

The basic plot of the film revolves around a small Iowa farmer, played by Kevin Costner, who is instructed by a strange voice to build a baseball diamond in the middle of his cornfield. The farmer is a huge baseball fan, so he builds the field. After it is complete, legendary baseball players from times gone by mysteriously begin gathering there to play ball, entering from between the tall corn stalks that rim the outfield. Among the players appears the farmer's father. Due to a fractured relationship, the farmer has never gotten to know him. At the climax of the movie, the farmer and his father start to play catch together for the first time.

I enjoy this movie and had seen it a couple of times before the boys were born, but it struck me very differently this time. As the farmer and his father did something as simple as playing catch, I "crashed" again, realizing that I would never know the joy of playing catch with my sons. I quickly left the room so they wouldn't see me crying.

ℂ

On a recent Sunday morning, I was sitting with my family at our Church, Grace Community, in Tempe, Arizona. As we listened to the service, Dylan interlocked his fingers with mine. I was already feeling a bit "down" from my inability to see the words to the songs of worship. Since I never memorized the words, I can't sing the verses.

As we sat there holding hands, listening to God's word, I started thinking about how large his hands had become. I looked down for a glimpse of something I couldn't see. I then began feeling his hand with my free hand. I felt his thumb and was surprised at how large his thumbnail had gotten. I then felt his fingers, his knuckles and his fingertips. He must have thought I was behaving rather oddly, but he didn't pull away.

I then began to think about how unfair it was that I couldn't even see my own son's hand. This hand, which for the past ten years has been in clear view to everyone, was something I would never see. Right then I began to 'lose it' again. Fortunately, this time my tears were silent, and I don't think Dylan knew I was crying.

It has been very important to me that my sons never see me get upset about my blindness. I have always thought that if they perceived that it was difficult for me, they would somehow be burdened, too. In general, I'm not one of these macho guys who thinks he can't let his sons see him cry, but when it comes to my blindness, it seems, things are different.

ʕ

During a recent ski trip with Dino Paul, I was faced with yet another cruel reminder of things that would never be. Sitting at lunch in the day lodge, we were catching our breath and enjoying our meal, waiting for Dino's wife, Jenny, and their 12-year-old daughter, Natalie, due to arrive from Phoenix.

Dino innocently commented that Natalie was absolutely fearless on the slopes and that she would wear him out the next day when they would ski together. I began thinking that Colton would be exactly like that. I could picture him skiing all over the slopes, with me trying to keep up with him. It was, of course, just a dream. I would never get to see Colton skiing. I would never get to chase him all over the hill. Before the accident, I had envisioned myself teaching my boys how to ski and spending countless weekends on the slopes with them on father/son trips. "Now it simply isn't going to happen," I thought, almost aloud.

As I sat there with Dino, it was all I could do not to lose it. But I didn't want him to know I was upset. I held my breath to keep my shoulders from shaking. After all, it wasn't his fault; it was just that reality sucks sometimes. I pretended to eat to avoid having to engage in any conversation, but eating was the last thing I felt like doing. Trying to appear busy, I sipped my drink and stirred my soup.

In a matter of minutes, the sadness passed and I regained my composure. But for those few minutes I couldn't talk. I think Dino realized what was going on and understood that no words would make a difference. So he remained silent. Thanks, Dino.

Another thought I occasionally have is, "What was my last basketball game at the club like? How did I play? Who was on my team and who did I play against? Did I have a great game, a bad game or was it just an average game? What if I had known it was my last basketball game, my last turn around jumper, my last move to the right?" Hypothetical questions, but interesting nonetheless.

&

I sometimes have regrets about things I didn't see enough of or didn't see at all. If I had known I was going to lose my sight one day, I would have spent less time sitting in traffic and more time watching sunsets or hiking the desert.

Near the top of the list of my regrets is that I never saw the Grand Canyon. It's hard to imagine, isn't it? I am a second generation Arizonian and I never visited this place which is considered one of the greatest wonders of the world. It's almost unpatriotic. And to make it worse, at one time, when I was in my early 20s, I lived in Sedona, Arizona, not two hours from the canyon. Unfortunately, I was always too busy with other things I thought were more important.

I need to pass the lesson from this on to you, the reader. If there's something you want to see or do, see it, do it! Live each moment today instead of waiting for tomorrow.

&

The most critical of my regrets is that I didn't start my family earlier. Missing out on all of the sights that go along with our sons' growing up is certainly one of the most difficult 'misses' I have had to overcome. Events that I am better off not thinking about include: not being able to see my sons sleeping in their cribs; not being able to see them playing in their kiddy pool; not being able to see them, scrubbed and jauntily outfitted, on their first day of school; not being able to see their faces on Christmas mornings; and not actually *seeing* them suited up in their baseball uniforms. Sure, it's futile to look back to all of the 'wasted' time I spent doing things that I thought were important. At the time, those things *were* important. But still, I go there from time to time, unbidden, and think thoughts like, "If I could only trade one day I wasted watching TV for one day watching my boys."

One of my biggest fears today is that I will forget what people look like. I worry that inactivity in my visual cortex will cause me to slowly lose the ability to store visual images. I have no medical or scientific proof that this phenomenon occurs in the brain, but my own perceptions give me some anecdotal evidence. Looking back to people I knew 20 or 30 years ago, I do not have a clear picture in my mind of what they looked like. While I might recognize them on a street corner if I was able to see them today, I don't have a vivid memory of the details.

The reason this worries me is that the thought of forgetting what my beautiful wife looks like is too hard to bear. And I can't imagine a time when I would forget what my mom, dad, brother or sisters look like. It is a dark place in my mind that, thankfully, I do not visit often.

The good news is that I do have a clear picture of them now, and I incorporate that into my everyday life, taking a moment or two each day just to visually remember them. (By the way, everyone looks just as good as they did in 1994, and Kristi never has a bad hair day).

Generally speaking, I don't waste a lot of time lamenting over lost opportunities. I do my very best to live in the present, not in the past. I enjoy whatever I can do with the senses I have. God has blessed me with the proverbial "glass is half full" philosophy. I am a firm believer that you get out of life what you put into it. I hope I will be remembered as a guy that went through some hard knocks but kept a positive mental attitude and came out the other side.

Part Six:

"... and I will dwell in the house of the Lord forever."

Chapter 31

Kristi . . . "til death do us part."

amily and friends close to me, as well as astute acquaintances, realize very quickly that one of the primary reasons for my success is my incredible wife, Kristi. She has been there for me on so many levels since our accident that, at times, I almost take her for granted. Almost.

To begin with, the fact she stayed with me after I became blind is a huge statement in and of itself. She will tell you that there was never a time that she considered anything else, that when you love someone you stick by them. But, statistically speaking, that doesn't appear to be the norm. In fact, a majority of couples today face the trauma of divorce.

I honestly believe that if Kristi had left me a year or two after the accident, no one would have blamed her. They would have given her credit for hanging in there as long as she did and would have understood her leaving a tough situation.

What she actually did was the exact opposite. She stood by her man "'til death do us part"—not to be a martyr, or because she felt obligated to do so, but because she loved me regardless of my limitations. As cliché as it sounds, I was the same person inside, and I have come to believe that she saw the old Steve, the one she fell in love with from the start.

Not only did she pledge her unwavering support from the beginning, she chastised me for even suggesting that she opt for the easy way out. Yes, I actually did that at one point. One day, several months after I got home from the hospital, I *decided* that it would be best if she left me. I suggested that she move back to Missouri where she could be close to her family for support. I was in a deep depression, and I was convinced that I no longer had the capacity to be an effective father or husband. I was blind. What good would I be to anyone? I felt that the burden of taking care of me would be too much for her to handle.

When I told her about my decision, Kristi responded very sternly. "I never want to hear you talk like that again. I am in this for the long haul, whatever that brings. Understand?"

That was the last conversation we had on the topic. When Kristi vowed at our wedding to stay with me through good times and bad, in sickness and in health, she really meant it.

In July of 2002, Kristi returned with me to that Tropicana island wedding chapel to renew those wedding vows of a decade earlier. This time I couldn't see my beautiful bride as she walked down the aisle. But the moment was more emotionally charged than the first time she did it. In front of a crowded chapel of family, friends, and our miracle sons, she repeated her lifelong commitment to stay with me through good times and bad, in sickness and in health, 'til death do us part. Everyone in that chapel knew that she had not only 'talked the talk, but that she had already 'walked the walk'. Once again I thought: 'What in the world did I ever do to deserve such an incredible bride?'

Over the years, Kristi has been my biggest supporter, my best friend, my confidant and my soul mate—the wind beneath my wings. She has been there to love me through the tough times and to celebrate the victories. Without her belief in what I could accomplish, I would not have had the confidence to push on.

Since that terrible day in April of 1994, Kristi has continued to amaze me with what she has been able to accomplish for herself and on her own. Besides being a loving and involved Mom, and nursing her husband back from the brink of physical and mental despair, she has managed to be very successful in her own career.

Her first venture back into the working world after the accident was a return to her job as a pharmaceutical sales representative. She had always enjoyed this challenging work and was anxious to get back to calling on doctors and hospitals. After a few weeks back on the job, however, it quickly became apparent this career path was no longer a viable option. The job required her to spend a lot of time on her feet, and with the damage done to her foot in the accident she was physically incapable of standing up for hours at a time and walking on it all day.

As it turned out, for Kristi, a limitation opened the door for an opportunity. "A blessing in disguise," she says. Her apparent limitation forced her to re-evaluate her career, and to pursue a different path which, as she puts it, "is even more rewarding."

Ever since I met Kristi, I was always aware of how comfortable people felt sharing their personal stories with her. In the span of a few minutes, they would tell her about their problems and ask for her opinion. There is no doubt that she is blessed with the gift of empathy.

One day, a cable TV technician came over to our home to fix our TV. I left the room for a few minutes, and when I returned he was telling Kristi all about his deteriorating marriage and how difficult it was on his children. It was as though she was wearing a sign that read, "Tell me. I care." I didn't 'get it' at first, because the sign I was wearing said, "Please fix my TV and leave ASAP."

When the boys were three years old and our lives had settled down somewhat, Kristi returned to college to get her masters degree in counseling. After two and a half years of balancing her busy home life with her heavy academic schedule (and some acting and modeling on the side!), she graduated—with honors.

She did her internship at the Arizona Center for the Blind and Visually Impaired (ACBVI). At that time, I was serving as the President of the Board of Directors and Bill Clinton was the President of the United States. I would jokingly tell people that I was definitely having relations with an intern.

In 2001, Kristi opened her private practice. Among other issues, she does family grief work, adolescents, and couple's counseling. She is truly gifted at what she does and now gets to help people every day. She has loved it from the very first day. And it wasn't long before I realized that I was no longer the only Welker 'in demand'.

One day, when I was going to do a presentation at a senior citizens' facility in Scottsdale, I asked Kristi to tag along. I gave my usual speech about how I became blind and what I have done to overcome the disability, and there was polite applause. Kristi then discussed the psychological implications of being disabled and what it is like to live with a disabled person and be the caregiver. For the next 45 minutes, I sat quietly and listened as the audience peppered Kristi with questions asking her advice on a number of issues. I felt like I was just the warm-up act.

In her spare time—which today is almost nonexistent—she writes practical advice articles for a local newspaper and conducts seminars on grief and resiliency. And as if that's not enough, she has gone on to complete her Doctor of Psychology degree. When friends tease and ask if she insists that I call her Dr. Welker, I tell them that I already call her that, and I do it with a great deal of pride. In my humble opinion, she is the best psychologist in town. I think her patients would agree.

Sometimes I just shake my head at what this unbelievable woman has been able to accomplish under such difficult and often traumatic circumstances. Who knows what is next for her—maybe putting an end to world hunger or something? All I know is that I am sure lucky to have this angel in my life. I also strongly recommend that, if you are going to suffer a brain injury, it's a good idea to be married to a psychologist.

Chapter 32

The Missed Bachelor Party

On the night of our accident, April 30, 1994, I was supposed to attend a bachelor party for Jeff Pawlowski, a good and loyal friend whom I liked and respected immensely. Obviously, I never made it to the party. I have always felt badly that our accident cast a cloud over the event. But thinking back to that time always reminds me of a memorable incident that occurred about a week earlier. The event holds a special place in my memory, since it was one of the last things I saw.

Kristi and I were having lunch at a restaurant in Scottsdale called Pichkes. While we were dining, we began to talk about Jeff's upcoming party. Kristi told me in no uncertain terms that she did not want me going to any strip clubs. Quite innocently, I told her that I had not planned the party and could not control where it went.

One thing led to another and it developed into a major disagreement. It was a silly argument, at best, because I really didn't have strong feelings one way or another about going to the strip club. Unfortunately, the conversation rapidly escalated into a heated debate. Kristi finally got so upset with me that she stood up and stormed out of the restaurant. The only problem was we were nowhere near our home. I figured that she would be waiting for me outside. So, I paid the bill, stepped outdoors, and was surprised to see that Kristi wasn't there. Of course, I thought, she's waiting in the Jeep. But she wasn't there either. I climbed into the SUV and started out on a trek to find her. Driving down Scottsdale Road, a busy street by the restaurant, I finally saw her. She was stomping down the sidewalk, looking as mad as a wet hornet. As she was walking against traffic, I could not pull up next to her so I pulled into the left turn lane and slowed down to match her walking pace. She totally ignored my presence, choosing to stare straight ahead.

Who knows where she thought she was going—but she was clearly determined to get there quickly.

I yelled to her several times, saying how sorry I was. No luck. Then I began pleading with her in a mournful voice, admitting that I had been a jerk and begging for her forgiveness. Cars began honking at me as I continued my pitiful pleas at less than five miles per hour on the busy thoroughfare. Eventually, after what seemed like an eternity in time, with a concerto of car horns in the background, I could see a smile cracking on her face.

"I hate it when you make me laugh when I'm mad at you!" she finally said as she faced me, tears rolling down her cheeks and disappearing into her big smile. I pulled into the nearest parking spot, got out of the Jeep, and we embraced. I held her tightly as I apologized for my behavior. Man, I can be a real jerk sometimes.

At the time, this seemed like such a major ordeal. If I had known what lay in store for the following week, I think I would have utilized this time more constructively. Time: a precious commodity that we can never get back.

Chapter 33

Overcoming Grief

Perhaps the one skill I have mastered better than any other is overcoming grief. This is certainly not a skill I aspired to, nor was it one I thought I would ever need to master. But out of necessity, I have done so.

An interesting observation I made while overcoming my grief is realizing that I am not alone. As I have moved forward through the years, I have become more aware and more empathetic of people who are dealing with their own grief.

Before my tragedy, I mostly steered clear of people struggling with grief. It was as though they had the plague and I thought I was going to catch it. Furthermore, I incorrectly reasoned, there was nothing I could say or do to help the situation. I worried that by saying something, I might make matters worse.

For whatever reason, those who experience grief seem to belong to an exclusive club. As members of that club, we share our grief, knowing that we will not be ostracized or judged.

It's like we have all visited the same foreign country (or maybe served in the same war). And only those who have been there can understand the emotional impact. Maybe it is more like we are refugees or former prisoners of war and we can only commiserate with people who have been through what we have been through. Regardless of the reasons, it is something only those of us who have suffered can understand.

Dr. Elisabeth Kubler-Ross lists the five stages of grief as: denial;, anger; bargaining; depression; and acceptance. While the model was developed for those who are experiencing death, many psychologists use this model for the stages of grief. In situations like mine, I believe this model applies. Quite simply, I suffered the death of my old life.

What I have learned about the model is this: it is not a straight road with predetermined stops at each stage. While I spent my fair share of time in denial (initially, I couldn't even say the word "blind"), I made only a brief stop at anger. Being the logical, left brained person that I am, I didn't see much value in the bargaining stage, either. The depression level, on the other hand, felt like an extended layover.

Even though I now live in acceptance, it doesn't mean that I don't, on occasion, take a trip back to the other stages. Through my experience, I now know that healing can take a lifetime. There is always more to say, always more to write.

Grief recovery has followed a fairly simple formula for me; I focused in on who I was before my accident; who I am now; what I have learned; how I was going to get past the loss and what I wanted my future to be.

I have found that people traumatized by grief get there from many places. What may be an inconsequential event to one person may be an overwhelming obstacle to another. I have also learned not to judge someone else's grief by some personalized scale of severity. In other words, I don't sit back and think; 'This person has only been through a minor trauma, they shouldn't be so upset.' I am convinced that no matter how you get there, grief is grief.

I have also learned that there are many myths about grief. Among those I heard on a regular basis were: God doesn't give you more than you can handle; time heals all wounds; just keep busy and replace the loss. Understanding that these were, in fact, myths helped me in my healing process.

There is an example that goes like this: If you take a group of people and have them throw all of their troubles into the center of the room and tell them that they can exchange them for any of the other troubles that are lying there . . . they will most often take back their own!

As odd as this may sound, that is certainly the case for me. Faced with this choice, I would leave the room with my blindness. I have learned to deal with this disability. And I truly feel blessed in the life that I lead. Am I saying that it is an easy life? No, not at all. Rather, it's that God has given me a few wonderful personal attributes: patience, tenacity and perseverance. This has helped me to put my life back together and find a purpose . . . to reach a stage of existentialism. I have been able to answer the question: what is the meaning of my life?

Chapter 34

"No Rancho Yeto"

During the summers when I was young, my sister Janice and I spent considerable time with our grandparents in a dusty little town called Bowie, Arizona, a place which has long been passed over, thanks to the decline in passenger train travel and the completion of a major interstate. Although, past its prime, Bowie still had a lot of character and charm.

My folks were raised there, and the place is loaded with childhood memories. It has all of the features you'd expect in small town America. There's a community pool, a family grocery store, a couple of small efficiency motels, and a Dairy Burger. Janice and I would spend several weeks each summer learning the ways of rural life. For city kids like us, that was an eye opening experience.

On our visits, we would spend time at both our maternal and paternal grandparents' homes. This was an interesting dichotomy. Our grandparents couldn't have been more different, even if they'd lived a world apart.

Ira and Pauline Welker were very proper, conservative people and their home was a well-organized one. Their place, from a child's point of view, seemed more like a museum. Everything was in its place and a strict schedule was the order of the day—every day. The high point of a visit was having prune juice for breakfast.

My maternal grandparents' place, on the other hand, was the exact opposite. Skeets and Lois Thomas's home was always a vortex of confusion and chaos, with people coming and going at all hours of the day and night. You never knew who would be stopping by for a meal. There was "stuff" everywhere, and my Grandma's kitchen counters were always piled high with canning supplies. She was always preserving something, and you never quite knew what she was going to feed you next.

The two-block walk from one home to the other would take us from one world to another. But, we always felt loved and cared for in both homes. I must say, though, that the Thomas home was by far the more entertaining place for little kids to be.

The most exciting part of my visits was spent helping Grandpa Skeets at his bar, Skeets' Tavern. The doors to this community landmark opened some time in the 1930s, but no one is around today to verify the exact date. It probably would have been a historic site had it not been a tavern. Skeets operated the place until he was 95 years old. It was ironic that he ran a tavern. He was a recovering alcoholic, but I didn't understand all of that when I was young. I was only allowed in the tavern in the early morning, before he opened for business. He would have me sweep the floors, re-stock coolers and perform various light duties suited to a little boy. And after my work was done, he would reward me with a Coke, beef jerky, cherries, and pickled eggs (a combination you couldn't pay me to eat today). He also paid me with silver dollars, but that didn't seem too important to me at the time, at least not when compared to the snacks. Some mornings, when Grandpa Skeets finished his work with a little time to spare before the noon opening hour, he would teach me to play pool on the tavern's pool table. He'd also give me nickels to put into the jukebox to play my own favorites. For a little kid, I was living large.

Before we started each morning's chores at the tavern, we would make a stop at a place Grandpa Skeets called "No Rancho Yeto." This was my Grandpa's slang Spanish name for his small ranch, and small it was, consisting of a little corral, one or two horses, and a few 'lean' chickens.

Today, I look back on "No Rancho Yeto" with a bit of sadness. I think ranching was his true passion, but he never pursued it. Skeets lived until he was 95 years old, but I'm not sure he fulfilled his dream; found his purpose.

As I close in on my 50th birthday, I sometimes wonder if my best years are behind me. I can no longer deny that I teed off on the back nine some time ago. Like many Americans, maybe I peaked in my 30's or 40's.

But, I'd like to think that my best years are yet to come. For inspiration, I need look no further than my dad. When he was my age, he was retiring from a successful banking career of more than 20 years. But he wasn't done yet. Soon after leaving the bank, he went into the insurance business and ran an agency for 15 years. He also opened and operated two restaurants, started three new insurance agencies, and opened a convenience store. At the time of this writing, Dad is 78 years old and, much to mom's chagrin, he shows no signs of slowing down.

Lessons learned from both my grandfather and my dad? *Define my passion and purpose in life and pursue it.*

I believe that life is 10% what happens to you and 90% what you, with God's help, do about it. I am determined not to get to the end of my days with "No Rancho Yeto."

Chapter 35

The Future's So Bright, I Gotta Wear Shades

My journey through life is certainly proving to be more, well . . . *interesting* than I would have envisioned. The auto accident was not even the first near-death experience of my life. My childhood was fraught with mishaps that could easily have ended my time on this earth prematurely. At the age of nine months, I developed pneumonia and had to live in an oxygen tent for a week. Until I reached the age of 5, I continued to scare my parents with death defying feats.

Before my third birthday had come and gone, I decided, while traveling in my Mom's car, to hop out the back door. I tumbled down a cinder embankment, suffering scrapes and contusions. After a second jump from the backseat, Mom came up with a brilliant idea (these were the days before seatbelts). She put a playpen in the back seat to confine my roaming until I got to an age in which I understood the dangers of leaping from a moving car.

My next trick, when I was about four, was to jump from the second story loft of the family cabin to the hard wood floor below. Not so lucky this time, I suffered a concussion and spent several days in the hospital.

On an outing to the Salt River Canyon, I again though leaping off of a high point looked like fun. So, I jumped off a ledge. Thankfully, there was a flat, sand outcropping ten feet below that cushioned my fall. Otherwise, I would have fallen a lot farther—and probably wouldn't have survived. As it turned out, I was not seriously hurt.

Not yet learning my lesson, I continued to be impulsive. I followed a puppy into the forest early one morning and was lost for most of the day. Almost every able-bodied citizen in the little town of Show Low,

Arizona, joined the search party. My brother Jim went door-to-door, bribing neighbors with Mom's cookies to enlist their help in the search. (Why Jim wasn't looking for me is still a mystery.)

According to my Mom, one of our neighbors had a "divine intervention" and told them where I might be. Sure enough, I was found at nightfall, much deeper in the forest than the search party had been looking—cold and wet, but otherwise in good shape.

For my final childhood act, just before I turned five, I fell off a horse and sustained a double fracture of my arm. Thankfully, I didn't land on my head!

Until recently, we viewed my experiences as simply the escapades of an overactive child, stories that eventually evolved into humorous family anecdotes recalled at holiday gatherings.

Now, however, I think there is a much deeper meaning to these 'near misses.' The fact that I survived not only my childhood mishaps but also my auto accident, clearly shows that there was a greater plan at work. Even a skeptic like me has to ask; "Why? Why am I still here?"

I think the answer is this: to help others understand that, no matter how dark the future may look, there is always light. One need look no further than my story to see that you can come out on the other side, and thrive.

Before the accident, I thought I had the world by the tail. I was young, talented and successful. What I lacked, however, was purpose and passion.

Today, through my motivational speaking and community work, I am able to touch thousands of people. It energizes me to know that my story helps others overcome challenges in their own lives. I like to tell people, "The future's so bright, I gotta wear shades!"

Epilogue

I hope it's abundantly clear that I give all of the credit for my recovery to the Lord. Left to my own devices and resources, I would never have been able to put my life back together and be the husband and father He wanted me to be. I shudder to think of the low place I would be today without His guidance and strength.

Before the accident, I was not a believer. I thought there was probably a God of some kind, but I didn't give it much more thought than that. I felt that I was basically in control of my own destiny. If there was a God, he was certainly not a God who had a personal interest in me. I guess you could say that I belonged to the Steve Welker religion, a belief system I had created myself.

Kristi has been a Christian for most of her life, and she played a critical role in my walk. After we married, she talked me into going to church sometimes. For the most part, I had no problem with the sermons, but I was still customizing and interpreting the messages to fit neatly into my preconceived notion of what Christianity should be. Once again, I was in *total control* and everything was running smoothly.

Don't misunderstand. I wasn't a bad person before I became a Christian. I wasn't on the road to self-destruction, finding Jesus in the nick of time. I wasn't addicted to drugs, alcohol, sex, or any of the other demons that rob so many of their lives. I was a good guy with good intentions. I was honest, hard working and reliable. I had my life micromanaged to the smallest detail. I believed I was in total control of my career, my family, my friends—everything! And that remained true for me right up until April 30, 1994, when my life was forever changed.

While some Christians can remember the exact time and place they became believers, that's not the case for me. I don't recall ever having a crystallized moment—an "enlightenment,"—when Jesus entered my life. Maybe it was because of the head injury I sustained, or maybe it was because of the pain medication I was prescribed. (Or could it be that it took a long time for the message to penetrate my thick skull?)

Regardless of when the exact moment of conversion was, one particular occasion stands out in my memory.

I was lying in bed at St. Joseph's Hospital a few weeks after the accident. Grace Community Church had been notified. A visitor from the church, Dick Keogh, came to the hospital to see me. I didn't know him and was seeing very few visitors. I don't even recall the details of our conversation, or the words of his prayer. But, I do remember how the prayer affected me. I felt an incredible weight being lifted off my shoulders, and I thought, "God is here for me. I will not have to deal with this devastating tragedy on my own. I have someone to carry me. His name is Jesus Christ."

Once out of the hospital, as my health permitted, Kristi and I began regularly attending church. With our fragile health and our newborn babies, we found it was a major ordeal. But, we tried to attend every week.

I pushed myself because I was motivated. In fact, Sunday quickly became the most important day of the week for me. I sat there in my dark world with my wife and new babies and soaked in the Pastor's words.

I am sometimes asked if I think God caused my accident to get my attention. The answer is, I honestly don't know. What I do know is that he either caused it or allowed it to happen, and it doesn't really matter which. I know that God picked me up and carried me through the valley of the shadow of death because my time on this Earth was not yet finished. He gave me hope by healing my body and my mind; He gave me vision through salvation and He gave me purpose with the gift of sharing my message to help others.

Thankfully, it doesn't take a genius to see what God's purpose for me is. I am certainly not a 'head-smart' Christian. I can't quote chapter and verse from the Bible. I am, however, a 'heart-smart' Christian, a believer who sees the power of God at work in my life everyday.

I believe God allowed me to live so that I can finish the work He has for me. While I am not sure of the entire plan, I know that sharing my story to help others is part of it. He has given me the gift of communication, both written and verbal. I believe He wants me to share with people the good news that anything is possible, with His help.

The most important part of my life today is my walk with the Lord, Jesus Christ. Prior to 1994, I was a lost soul with no life beyond the mortal one. I lived for no one but myself. Now, I will not perish, but will have eternal life (John 3:16).

This is not to say that I am perfect now. Far from it. I still struggle with sin and work everyday to improve myself. I know there is an instruction manual called the Bible, along with a Holy Spirit to guide me along the way.

I truly believe I have more blessings now than I did when I could see. My marriage to Kristi, the most amazing, supportive person I have ever met, has blossomed into a stronger relationship than I could have ever dreamed. Although it is often overused in our culture today, the term "soul mate" certainly applies.

I have been blessed with, in my humble opinion, the two greatest boys on the face of the planet. The intense feelings of joy, pride, happiness and, yes, even worry and frustration, are emotions that can only be understood by a parent. I am excited to see the great works God has planned for them.

In 2002, I was baptized. I was first baptized as a child, but I didn't understand the meaning and significance of the ceremony. The Bible commands us to be baptized, and that was good enough for me.

I asked Dr. Travis Holcombe to baptize me. He had put my body back together after the accident and had played an important role in my physical life. More importantly, God had used Travis to help lead me to Christ, and eternal life.

That evening was very special to me because my sister, Janice who had recently become a follower of Christ, joined me and was also baptized. The strong, spiritual emotions I felt that evening are ones I'll never forget.

I told those gathered, "Prior to my accident, I could see the world but was blind to the ways of the Lord. I am now physically blind but clearly see Him, and He leads my way."

As the program ended, Gary Bloomquist, the music director at East Valley Bible Church, stood up and began singing a beautiful solo rendition of "Amazing Grace." He probably does this at the end of every baptismal service, but I felt that he was singing directly to me:

Amazing grace, how sweet the sound
That saved a wretch like me.
I once was lost, but now I'm found.
Was blind, but now I see.

About the Author

S ince this entire book is about Steve Welker—his life, his challenges and his triumphs, there is not much to say that hasn't already been said. Yet, some details remain, and this is the place for them.

In 1980, Steve Welker graduated from Arizona State University with a bachelor's degree in business and a field of specialization in insurance. He completed the Westfield Basic Insurance School in 1982 and is a Certified Insurance Councilor (C.I.C.). Steve is the President and founder of Universal Business Insurance of Arizona.

He is the current President of the Board of Directors for the Arizona Center for the Blind and Visually Impaired (ACBVI) and Chairman of Welker Charities, a not for profit fund raising corporation. He is also a spokesman for the United Way.

Steve lives in Phoenix, Arizona with his wife, Dr. Kristina Welker, a psychologist, their two sons, Colton and Dylan, and the family's three Pomeranians, Corky, Teddy and Tinkerbelle (who *really* runs the house!).

ß

Copies of this book are available on Steve Welker's web site:
http://www.worldatmyfingertips.com

Printed in the United States
130275LV00003B/1/A